RAZZLE DAZZLE QUILTS

JUDY HOOWORTH

Martingale
& COMPANY

WOODINVILLE, WASHINGTON

DEDICATION

To my grandmother, Olive May Armstrong Bibb (1882–1923), whose quilt I treasure;
and to my mother, Mavis Janet Wilshire Bibb Ellis.

• • •

ACKNOWLEDGMENTS

I am indebted to Karen Fail for her encouragement. Without her help this book would never have been written.

My grateful thanks to Anna Brown for typing the manuscript; Kerry Adams from Redmill Cottage for her excellent custom machine quilting; Jennifer Price, who helped with piecing; and Karen Fail, Jane Gibson, Sue Rowles, and Carolyn Sullivan, who loaned their fabulous quilts to me for inclusion in this book.

CREDITS

President . . . . Nancy J. Martin
CEO/Publisher . . . . Daniel J. Martin
Associate Publisher . . . . Jane Hamada
Editorial Director . . . . Mary V. Green
Editorial Project Manager . . . . Tina Cook
Technical Editor . . . . Laurie Baker
Copy Editor . . . . Ellen Balstad
Design and Production Manager . . . . Stan Green
Illustrator . . . . Robin Strobel
Cover and Text Designer . . . . Trina Stahl
Photographer . . . . Brent Kane

That Patchwork Place is an imprint of
Martingale & Company.

Razzle Dazzle Quilts
© 2001 by Judy Hooworth

Martingale & Company
20205 144th Ave. NE
Woodinville, WA 98072-8478 USA
www.martingale-pub.com

Printed in Hong Kong
06 05 04 03 02 01   8 7 6 5 4 3 2 1

MISSION STATEMENT

We are dedicated to providing quality
products and service by working together to inspire
creativity and to enrich the lives we touch.

Library of Congress Cataloging-in-Publication Data

Hooworth, Judy.
    Razzle dazzle quilts / by Judy Hooworth
    p.   cm.
    ISBN 1-56477-322-1
    1. Patchwork. 2. Quilting. I. Title.

TT835.H556259 2001
746.46'041—dc21
                                        00-052192

CONTENTS

INTRODUCTION

AUSTRALIA IS A land of startling colors and vivid contrasts, from the broad expanses of the vast Outback, with its red earth and cobalt sky, to the coastal fringes where the gray-green color of the bush reveals the red-purple twigs of the eucalypts. There are also the jewel colors of the surf and sand, and the ever-changing hues of our cosmopolitan cities.

I live a half hour north of Sydney, a city built around a spectacular harbor spanned by the famous Sydney Harbour Bridge and home of one of the world's most outstanding buildings, the Sydney Opera House. My home is in Terrey Hills, a "bush" suburb on the edge of Kuringai National Park—15 minutes from the most beautiful beaches in the world. Our flowers and birds contain all the colors of the rainbow. In fact, a very noisy visitor to my garden is the rainbow lorikeet.

It is from this colorful environment that I draw the inspiration for my quilts. Here, there are black-and-white currawongs, crimson rosellas, red-and-green king parrots, sulphur crested cockatoos, and pink and gray galahs, to name just a few of the birds that frequent my garden. In the gardens and the bush close by, there are pink boronia and waxflower, yellow wattle, golden banksia, and red grevilleas. The greens of the bush are ever-changing. Occasional bush fires leave a bluish haze and a stark, blackened landscape. And then there are the colors of the sky, the sand, the surf . . . .

To this colorful palette, add the patterns of nature—the scribbly lines on the trunk of a gum tree, the dense linear petals of the banksia flower and the jagged outline of its leaves. Contrast these with the grids and geometric patterns of the urban environment: roads, bridges, buildings, and construction.

I love working with bright, bold, intense colors, and I enjoy using printed fabrics with strong linear elements. I am excited by the chance juxtaposition of the two, and this forms the basis of all my work. Because color and print are the main features of my quilts, the structure is kept simple. I build up a quilt with small units and, as I enjoy the creative process, I work intuitively, with each step dictating the next. Decision making is part of the fun!

The quilts in this book are based on squares, rectangles, and traditional pieced blocks. These blocks are expanded by "splitting" them (sometimes more than once) and adding sashing and joining squares. Thus, I obtain a complex look by building up a design from simple components. Much of the apparent complexity, however, is determined by the choice of patterned fabrics. I use a large range of fabrics from each color family, which adds to the richness and texture of the surface. Fifty different reds are more exciting to use than two or three!

I have arranged the chapters in this book to reflect the processes I use when making a quilt. First, get your tools and supplies together and learn the basics of rotary cutting and piecing. Then, make color and fabric selections. For me, color inspiration usually comes first and then I decide how I will use it, looking at ideas for developing the quilt and trying various color combinations.

Allowing time to play with fabrics and to try out various combinations is vital to the creative process, so I am always experimenting. Fabric is no good if it remains uncut on the shelf because it is "too good to use." If you want, turn your experimental pieces into fantastic floor cushions or small quilts so that nothing really goes to waste.

I encourage you to read through the instructional chapters first to acquaint yourself with the progressive steps used to create a final product. The information presented in those chapters will help you better understand how to accomplish the Razzle Dazzle effect, and you will see photos of finished quilts that I hope will inspire you to eventually design your own Razzle Dazzle quilts. In the meantime, the instructional chapters are followed by ten projects for you to stitch so you can experiment with the techniques you learn. Have fun!

TOOLS AND SUPPLIES

- **Adjustable table lamp**

- **Design wall.** A vertical surface for designing enables you to see the development of your quilt at each stage of the design and to play with the arrangement. If you have wall space you can use, cover it with a piece of flannel or thin batting. Make the surface as taut as possible. If wall space is limited, create your own moveable panels by cutting a piece of plywood or foam-core board as large as space allows and covering it with flannel or batting as described above for the wall. Store the panels when they're not in use.

- **Drafting supplies (optional).** If you want to draft your own blocks, you will need graph paper, a pencil, a ruler, and an eraser.

- **Fabric.** Refer to "Fabrics with Fizz" on page 13.

- **Iron and ironing board**

- **Notebook and camera.** Keep these items handy for recording ideas and inspirations as they occur.

- **Pins and needles.** Quilting pins are useful for matching seams and for use as markers. Keep a supply of various-size sewing machine needles on hand so you will always have the right size for the fabric and thread you are working with. A hand-sewing needle is required to stitch the binding down, and if you plan to hand quilt, you will also need a Between quilting needle.

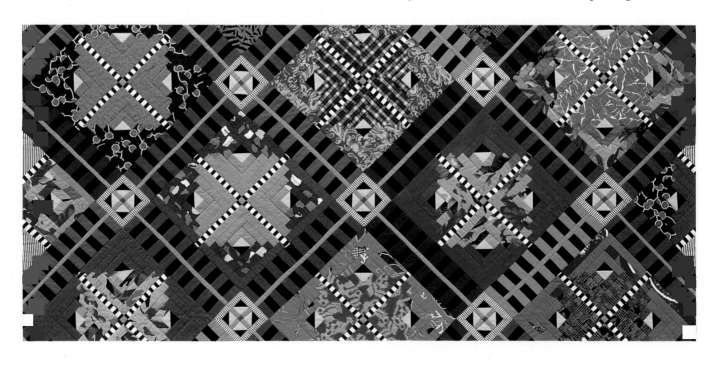

- **Rotary cutter, clear acrylic rulers, and self-healing mat.** There are many brands of rotary-cutting equipment available. I prefer to use a rotary cutter with a 1¾"-diameter blade and a mat no smaller than 12" x 18". Choose rulers that are marked clearly with ⅛" intervals. A 6" x 24" ruler is ideal for long cuts, while a 6" x 12" ruler works well for shorter cuts. A 6" square ruler is also useful for trimming pieced squares. Be sure to also have replacement blades on hand for your rotary cutter. As soon as the blade does not cut cleanly through the fabric, replace it.

- **Scissors and thread snips.** If you choose not to rotary cut the pieces, you will need a pair of good-quality scissors for cutting fabric, plus another pair of scissors for cutting out the templates. For both template and rotary-cutting methods, use thread snips or a pair of sharp, small scissors to clip threads.

- **Seam ripper**

- **Sewing machine.** A basic straight stitch machine is all you need for piecing the quilts. Keep your machine in good working order. Clean and oil it frequently, and change the needle often.

- **Tape measure**

- **Template-making supplies (optional).** If you prefer to work with templates rather than rotary cut the pieces, you will need template plastic and a marking pencil.

- **Thread.** An all-purpose thread in a medium gray or medium violet color is very versatile and will blend with most fabric colors.

ROTARY-CUTTING INSTRUCTIONS

THE QUILTS in this book are designed for template-free rotary cutting, which involves cutting strips from fabric and then cutting the strips into smaller segments. Most of the block designs are based on squares and rectangles. When triangles are used, they are either one-half or one-quarter of a square. All rotary measurements include a ¼" seam allowance. Please note that the following diagrams shown are for right-handers. Reverse the layout if you are left-handed.

Preparing the Fabric

To prepare your fabric, follow these steps:

1. Fold the fabric in half lengthwise, aligning the selvages. Lay the fabric on the cutting mat with the fold of the fabric closest to you and the bulk of the fabric to your left.

2. Align the horizontal line of a long ruler with the fold of the fabric. Cut along the edge of the long ruler through both layers. Move to the opposite side of the table, or rotate the cutting mat so the bulk of the fabric is to your right. You are now ready to cut your fabric strips.

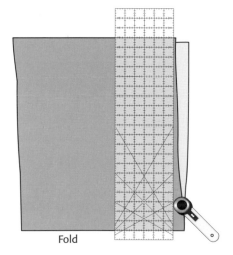

Fold

3. Repeat step 2 after approximately every three cuts to keep the fabric edge on grain.

Cutting Strips, Squares, and Rectangles

1. Place the ruler on the fabric. Line up the straight edge of the fabric with the line on the ruler that is the width of the strip you wish to cut. For example, if you need a 3"-wide strip, line up the 3" line on the ruler with the straight edge of the fabric and cut down the side of the ruler.

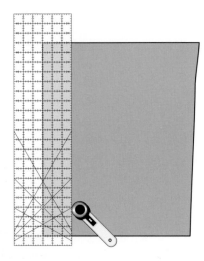

2. Turn the strip horizontally on the mat. Square up the strip ends in the same manner as the fabric edge. Be sure to remove the selvage edges.

3. Cut the strip into the desired-size squares or rectangles by aligning the line on the ruler that is the size you desire with the end of the fabric strip.

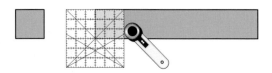

NOTE: *If you prefer to work with templates, draw the finished block size on graph paper and make templates from the completed design. For machine piecing, add a ¼" seam allowance around each shape.*

MACHINE PIECING

STANDARD ¼" seam allowances are used throughout this book. It is important to maintain an accurate seam allowance so the pieces will fit together properly. If you have a machine with a moveable needle position, set it so the needle stitches ¼" from the right side of the presser foot. If the needle is not moveable, measure ¼" to the right of the needle and mark the seam allowance on the sewing machine with a piece of masking tape. For many machines, a presser foot that measures ¼" from the needle to the outside edge is also available.

When piecing a number of units that are all the same, it will save time and thread if you chain piece. Place pieces to be joined right sides together, and pin as necessary. Feed the units under the presser foot, one after the other, without lifting the presser foot or clipping the connecting thread. When all of the units are pieced, clip the thread between the units.

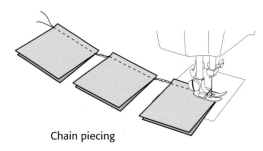

Chain piecing

COLOR, COLOR, AND MORE COLOR

WHAT IS IT that sets a Razzle Dazzle quilt apart from all the others? The secret is color—bold, bright, and brash. For quilters, color comes from fabric. Therefore, the more fabrics we have, the wider our color choices can be. In order to build a useful collection of fabrics, it is helpful to know a little more about color. Use the color wheel below to help you as we explore this colorful subject. Be sure to experiment with your fabrics in the various color schemes I discuss in this chapter. Be confident in your color choices, try some new ideas, and have fun!

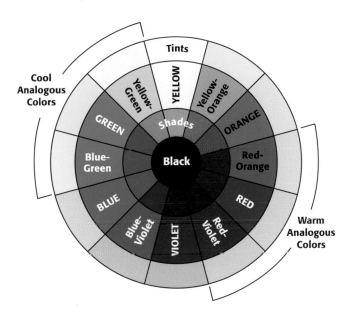

DESCRIBING COLOR

THERE ARE four main points to consider when talking about color—hue, value, intensity, and tone.

Hue

Hue is simply another name for color. For example, a red hue means the color red. The three primary colors or hues—red, yellow, and blue—can each be grouped into color families. For example, the red color family comprises all reds, such as crimson, scarlet, vermilion, strawberry, Venetian, cranberry, magenta, plum, ruby, rose, and russet. All the names we associate with red belong to this family. It is the same with the family of yellows and the family of blues. When pure red is mixed with pure blue in equal amounts, a secondary color—violet—is created. When more red is added it becomes a red-violet, and when more blue is added it makes a blue-violet. All these violets make up the violet color family. Red mixed with yellow makes another secondary color, orange (the orange color family), and yellow mixed with blue makes green (the green color family).

Where does brown fit in? The three primary colors mixed together make brown. The proportion of each primary color that is used will determine the color of brown. Brown is neutral, although it can be warm or cool. The brown color family contains the chocolate browns and all the beiges.

Black, white, and gray are also neutral colors. Pure black is the darkest dark and pure white is the lightest light. Fabrics that are predominately black but also contain lots of other colors are classified as black. Fabrics with white backgrounds or large areas of white in the print are considered white. When black and white are combined in one fabric, a strong visual contrast is created. These fabrics, when used in small amounts, will add zing to your quilt.

Value

When white is added to a color, it is called a *tint*. For instance, if you add white to pure red it makes pink. The more white that is added, the lighter the red becomes. Peach and apricot are tints or light values, of orange.

When black is added to a color, it is called a *shade*. Black added to red, for example, will make burgundy, which is a shade, or dark value, of red. Another example uses the color orange. Tans and rusts are the shades, or darker values, of orange.

Value scale of red and orange

Intensity

Intensity is the brightness of a color. On a value scale, the strongest color generally falls somewhere around the middle of the scale. The middle of the scale is where the color is the purest and most intense, such as the colors on the color wheel that are made up of equal amounts of pure color. When a color is diluted with black and white, it diminishes its brightness. As you move up and down the scale away from the pure color, the impact of the color is lessened. Therefore, when choosing colors for strong impact, *choose from around the middle range of the value scale.*

Tone

When gray is added to a color, it is called a *tone*. Grayed fabrics often have a muddy appearance. For example, mushroom pink, olive green, and teal blue are all tones. Some of the neutral beiges and grays also fit in this category. These colors do not sparkle like the clearer colors. While they are valuable additions to any fabric stash, they have limited use in Razzle Dazzle quilts.

DEVELOPING A COLOR SCHEME

CREATING A harmonious group of colors isn't hard when you use a color wheel to understand how the colors work together.

Monochromatic Color Scheme

The easiest color scheme is based on one color—a monochromatic scheme (*mono* means one and *chroma* means color). To illustrate, let's use the primary color red. As we have seen, red can vary in hue, value, intensity, and tone. To make an interesting and lively quilt, we need a good range of reds. Vary the hues, combining blue-reds and orange-reds, light reds and dark reds, dull reds and bright reds. Add high-contrast black and white for zing.

Cool-and-Warm Color Scheme

Draw an imaginary line that cuts the color wheel in half vertically from yellow to violet. All the colors on the left-hand side are cool colors. These are the colors of the oceans, sky, forests, and plants. They are restful colors and recede optically. The colors on the other side of the color wheel are warm colors. Warm colors are exciting and energetic. They are the colors of the sun and fire. Warm colors advance optically and demand our attention.

For example, red is a warm color. It can be used by itself, as we have seen, or its range can be expanded by adding related colors. Related colors are those that are side by side on the color wheel. Red-orange and orange, and red-violet and violet are all close to red on the color wheel. A few of these related colors added to the reds will add an extra dimension.

Analogous Color Scheme

Related colors are also known as analogous colors. An entire color scheme can be based around analogous colors. For example, if our red is a mid-value red, we could add shades of violet and tints of orange. Or we could use tints of violet, shades of red, and mid-values of orange (see "Force Field" on page 86).

A more complex color scheme can be achieved by expanding the range of related colors to include more of the neighboring colors. Of course, not all the colors will be used in equal amounts, equal values, or equal intensity (see "Sandy's Syncopation" on page 86).

To make your own color scheme, pick your favorite color on the color wheel. Look at its related colors and expanded warm or cool range. Note that the imaginary vertical line bisects the yellow and the violet. These two colors can be either cool or warm depending on the other colors you use with them. Yellow and violet are the two most useful colors in the spectrum because they will add sparkle and enhancement to other colors. They are also complementary colors (see right). They do not need to be at full strength to be effective. If the quilt lacks "oomph," add some yellow and/or violet. It always works. Medium violet and yellow ochre are also my most-used quilting thread colors because each blends with almost every combination of colors.

Refer to "Daintree" on page 70 for a cool color scheme that includes yellow and violet.

Triadic Color Scheme

Triadic (*triad* means three) is the name given to a color scheme that combines three colors that are equally spaced on the color wheel. Yellow, red, and blue are triads, as are orange, violet, and green. These colors can make a lively and exciting color scheme, particularly when used in their full intensity (see "Frog Court" on page 42, "Rosella Maze" on page 49, and "Composition in Red, Yellow, and Blue" on page 87).

Contrasting Color Scheme

When colors are warm, any cool color will contrast, and vice versa. The contrast will be very vibrant if the color is very intense, whereas the same color contrast in a diluted value will be more subtle. Contrasts work very well when used in small amounts; when used in equal amounts to the opposing colors, the dramatic effect of the contrast is lessened. See "Pink Fizz" (page 45) and "Floral Trellis" (page 87) for examples of warm/cool contrast, and "Blue Swimmers" (page 75) and "Soul Music" (page 88) for cool/warm contrast.

Complementary Contrast Color Scheme

Complementary colors are those directly opposite each other on the color wheel. A complementary color is a primary color with its opposite a secondary color (a mixture of the two other primaries). For example, red and green, orange and blue, and violet and yellow are all opposite colors. When placed next to each other, these colors intensify the brightness of each other. Put simply, orange will be enlivened by blue, green will be sparked by red, and violet will be jazzed up by yellow, and vice versa. When complementary colors are used at full strength and in equal amounts, the colors jump and vibrate together. The impact of the two colors can be altered depending on the value of each color and the proportion in which it is used (see "Blue Swimmers" on page 75).

Complementary contrast can also be used to draw attention to a specific area in the design. See the double-split sashing in "All That Jazz" on page 61. Note the proportions of the yellow and violet. Complementary contrast and cool/warm contrast can be achieved very easily without having to think too much about it. The secret is to add large, splashy prints to your collection. These prints, while being predominantly one color, will usually have touches of the complementary color included. When the fabrics are cut up and pieced into blocks, splashes of complementary color will occur throughout the quilt. Because the pattern is also irregular, you will have little control over the proportions of the color. This randomness can be visually exciting.

Splashy prints showing complementary contrast

Discordant Color Scheme

We all know it when we see colors that clash. When colors clash, it is called *color discord*. But discordant color combinations are also attention grabbers. When used in their full intensity next to each other, these combinations are visually exciting and stimulating. When diluted (a tint or a shade), the effect is not as dramatic but still creates interest. Discordant colors are separated on the color wheel but are not complements of one another. For example, red-orange and red-violet, yellow-green and orange, and blue and green are discords. You will see that these combinations can also be what I have called related colors. When you follow the ideas for color schemes I've suggested, discord is automatically included.

Polychromatic Color Scheme

Our color discussion began with a description of a monochromatic color scheme, which requires a collection of fabrics for a quilt based around one color. At the other extreme is a polychromatic color scheme that uses color from all over the color wheel (*poly* means many and *chroma* means color). Polychromatic schemes can be riots of color, especially when the colors are at their most intense (see "All That Jazz" on page 61 and "Razzle Dazzle" on page 91). Anything goes! High-contrast black and white will add vibrancy to the colors.

VARIETY IS THE key word to remember when choosing fabrics for a quilt. The wider the range of colors and prints in your fabrics, the more choices you can make. A good fabric stash will have lots of variety in all color families.

CHOOSING PRINTS

JUST AS there is an enormous range of value in fabric colors, there is an equally enormous range of prints to choose from. Aim to have a mixture of different types of prints, such as florals, geometrics, abstract prints, checks, polka dots, plaids, spots, linear patterns, and stripes. Stripes are a must in any collection. They contrast vividly with other prints and add sparkle to the design. Vary the scale of the prints; a mixture of small-, medium-, and large-scale prints is very useful and will add interest to your

quilts. Always look for large, splashy prints of any kind. These contrast very well with the more traditional prints and can look quite different depending on how they are cut. Don't forget solids, tone-on-tone prints, colorwash, and textured prints. Look for unusual color combinations and unusual designs. Don't overlook the dress fabric and decorator fabric suppliers. It's often in this group that you will find fabrics that are not mainstream. Choose bold and strong colors and prints; be adventurous in your selections.

Print is also important when developing a quilt around a specific theme—the prints you choose can help tell a story. In "Downtown" on page 88, rectangles of checks and plaids look like buildings with windows, while the bright colors suggest hustle and bustle, neon signs, and traffic lights. The prints in "Secrets of the Bush" on page 89 are a complete contrast. Here the prints are linear and organic, flowing, and as irregular as they are in nature. The prints tell a story of tree trunks and undergrowth, bark, twigs, and leaves.

SHOPPING FOR FABRIC

As YOU build your fabric stash, use the color wheel as a guide when you go to the fabric store. Stack the fabrics on shelves in color families, and then you can see at a glance the range of colors and patterns you have and the gaps that need filling. Shop selectively with your fabrics in mind. A broad range of color

Range of prints showing variety in pattern and scale

that you can tap into is more useful than a stash built around just a few colors. If you are just beginning to collect fabric, purchase ⅓ yard pieces. This way you can build up a good variety very quickly. Fat quarters can be useful, although I prefer the full-width cut because it's more versatile. I also choose cotton fabrics because they are easy to cut, they wear well, and they hold their shape. Sometimes I use a poly/cotton blend if the color and print are unusual. Always launder your fabrics before use.

STORING FABRICS

FABRICS SHOULD be protected from light, or they will fade over time. Plastic laundry baskets are useful for storing works in progress and can be moved around and stacked as necessary. Small, stackable, plastic containers are useful for storing scraps. Have one for each color family. These scraps are very useful when you want to audition a particular color for sashing or binding. I also have two containers for scraps that I cut into 1½" wide strips. One container is for light strips, and the other is for dark strips. I keep these especially for making Log Cabin quilts.

SQUARE DANCE: WORKING WITH SQUARES AND RECTANGLES

SQUARES AND RECTANGLES form the basis of almost all patchwork patterns. Very simple designs with squares and rectangles are often overlooked in favor of more intricate designs that show off a quiltmaker's piecing skills, yet simple arrangements of squares and rectangles can be turned into exciting quilts when many different fabrics are combined. Also, the more these shapes are subdivided, the more complex the designs become. In this chapter, I will show you how a wide range of fabrics with different prints, different patterns, and different values of one color will result in a quilt that is quite out of the ordinary.

WARM-UP EXERCISES

THE FOLLOWING exercises are designed to get your creative motor started. These exercises are not an end unto themselves; each piece can be enlarged or expanded to make a full-size quilt. Smaller pieces can be turned into small quilts or large floor cushions. See how some of these ideas have been developed in the projects on pages 41–85. These exercises build on each other, so be sure to follow them in the order given.

Exercise One

Refer to "Analogous Color Scheme" on page 11 to select two related colors from the color wheel. The colors can be warm or cool. Sort through your fabrics and see how many fabrics you can find in each of your chosen colors. Ideally, you will need twenty-five different fabrics from each color, but if you can't find that many, you can repeat some. This is where large-scale prints are very useful. Often they can be cut up to give a number of completely different pieces. Striped designs with varying stripe widths also will vary depending where the fabric is cut. Large abstract prints will do the same.

Sometimes a large print will have just two colors in almost equal amounts. For example, pink and yellow are two related warm colors. The fabric shown below could be used as either a pink with other pink prints or as a yellow with other yellow prints.

Print with two colors in equal amounts

Other prints may consist of two complementary colors in equal amounts. The print shown below can be combined with orange prints as an orange or with blue prints as a blue. The difference here is that a complementary contrast will occur automatically no matter which color family it is assigned to (refer to "Complementary Contrast Color Scheme" on page 11). If it is combined with other blue fabrics, the orange will appear in small amounts of color scattered over the quilt and vice versa—it's an eye catcher.

Print with two complementary colors in equal amounts

The important point to remember is that once you decide which color family a fabric should belong in for a particular project, it is necessary to keep it in that family and not use it in both groups.

Now look at the value (lightness and darkness) of your two color groups. Again, if you have a large amount of fabric, you can make choices about value. Your options for each group are to choose:

- All light
- All medium
- All dark
- A combination of light, medium, and dark
- A range of light to medium
- A range of medium to dark

You will notice that I haven't given the option of using light and dark fabrics together. A strong light/dark contrast is stark when used in large areas, creating too many hard andrigid lines at seams. I like the surface of the quilt to appear more fractured. Each area is broken up with large-scale prints and blending

values so that shapes are not so clearly defined. Keeping values within a close range enhances the depth of the color. If you choose the light, medium, and dark option, you will find the combination works better if most of your prints are mediums with just a few lights and darks added. Medium values contain the strongest color saturation. When mediums are combined, you get strong, vibrant color and intensity.

From each of the two color groups, cut 25 squares (50 total). Cut each square 4½" for a finished size of 4". A 4" square is perfect for small to large prints. Larger squares are too overpowering unless all your fabrics are very large-scale prints. Layer the fabrics and cut them with a rotary cutter, or make a template if you prefer.

Using your design wall, arrange each color group individually into five rows of five squares each. Don't make decisions about each fabric in relation to the next. Lay out the patches randomly (this is hard to do)! In the following photo examples, the pink prints are light to medium values, while the orange prints range from medium to dark.

Above, top: Arrangement of pink prints
Above, bottom: Arrangement of orange prints

Stand back and look at the arrangement. Move squares around only if you must. For example, if all the big, splashy prints are clumped together or all the darker values are in a regimented row, rearrange the squares for a more even distribution. Enjoy the randomness and the unexpected collision of different patterns.

NOTE: *It is not necessary to lay out the entire quilt, picking and choosing each square individually. If you cut each of your fabrics just once and put them on your design wall, you will be able to see if that group of fabrics works well together. If it does, you can confidently cut all the pieces for the entire quilt and sew them together randomly. The overall effect will be the same as your small sample.*

Look at the depth of color achieved by juxtaposing all the different fabrics. The variety of pattern also adds lots of interest for the eye. Note, too, how the large prints contain splashes of complementary color or cool/warm contrast. These fabrics add vibrancy; without them the arrangement loses its vitality. Remove the splashy prints from your arrangement and see the difference. See how the small areas of blue contrast with the pink fabrics in "Pink Fizz" (page 45) and the touches of blue contrast with the browns in "Secret Garden" (page 54).

Exercise Two

Combine your two color families from exercise one into a checkerboard arrangement. Make seven rows of seven squares each. You will have one square left over.

Pink and orange prints in a checkerboard arrangement

Immediately the result looks more complex and the depth of color has intensified. These two colors placed next to one another create a discord (refer to "Discordant Color Scheme" on page 12). This group of colors can be expanded for greater color depth by adding other related warm colors. Add some reds, violets, and yellows to the pinks and oranges. You can see the effect added colors have in "Rosella Maze" (page 49), where blues have been supplemented with violet, and the reds supplemented with peach or apricot.

Exercise Three

Squares can be broken up into smaller components to vary a design. Changing the proportions of the basic unit and adding a related shape, such as a rectangle, will make a more complex design. For this exercise, keep the squares from one of your color groups and cut the squares from the other color group into forty rectangles, each 2½" x 4½".

Now, let's add a zinger. Black-and-white fabrics contain the two extremes of contrast—the lightest light next to the darkest dark. Used in small amounts, black-and-white prints sparkle and add movement and rhythm to the quilt surface. Because black and white are neutrals, they can be used with any color. If your colored fabrics are bright lights, mediums, and darks, the denser blacks and whites will contrast very well. If your fabrics are very light or pale, the denser blacks and whites will contrast too much and become dominant. With paler fabrics, choose a black-and-white print with a more open pattern. For example, choose a narrow black stripe or black polka dot on white, or any fabric that has a white background with a fine black pattern printed on it. Choose a variety of black-and-white prints, and cut them into 2½" squares. Arrange them with the color squares and rectangles as shown in the photo on page 18.

These black-and-white squares provide a place for the eye to rest, although it doesn't linger because all the squares are different. Again, the large prints

Squares and rectangles with black-and-white zingers added

fracture the rigidity of the shapes. Refer to "Marella Polka" on page 89 to see how different this same design appears when all of the large color squares are cut from one fabric and the smaller squares are all cut from a different fabric.

Exercise Four

The proportions of the squares and rectangles can be altered to any size you choose. When the rectangles are narrow and in a contrasting color or value, they create a grid or lattice across the quilt surface.

Use the 4½" squares from one of the color groups. Choose a contrasting color in two values, and vary the scale of the two prints. If your fabrics are warm, choose a cool contrast, or vice versa. Cut the darker contrast print into 2" x 4½" rectangles and the lighter contrast print into 2" squares. Arrange the pieces on the design wall with the same arrangement from exercise three.

I chose a complementary contrast (blue) to the orange, with the blue being a darker value than the orange. When complementary colors are equal in value and intensity, the colors will appear to vibrate with one another, which can be very effective if you want a lot of movement. The squares I chose are a lighter value blue. In this arrangement, the effect is quite different from the previous example in exercise three. The design appears more ordered and more controlled than exercise three, yet at the same time the three design components create three points of interest. Orange is a warm color and advances, whereas blue is cool and recedes. However, here the blue grid has become the foreground with the orange in the background. The light blue squares dance their way across the surface and create a separate focal point. You can see a similar effect in "Rosella Maze" (page 49) and "Square Dance" (page 90), where the different blues advance and recede.

Exercise Five

Rectangles also make a good one-patch design, or they can be combined with squares or other rectangles of different sizes. In this example (still with the original color groups), the dominant feature of the design is created by the black-and-white stripes, which create a strong repetitive rhythm across the surface of the quilt. If you experiment with the stripe width, you'll find that bold black-and-white stripes approximately ⅜" wide create more movement than a narrow stripe.

Warm fabric squares and contrasting cool prints

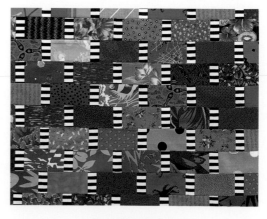

Repetitive rhythm

From each of the two color groups, cut twenty-five rectangles, each 3" x 5½", and ten squares, each 3" x 3". From the black-and-white stripe, cut four strips, each 1½" wide, across the width of the fabric; crosscut the strips into 3" segments. Arrange the rectangles on the design wall, alternating and separating the two colors with the black-and-white stripe. Each row will have a square at one end.

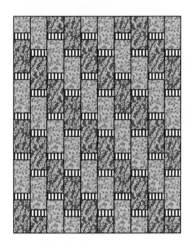

Vertical arrangement

"Downtown" (page 88) is constructed in this way, with striped rectangles of varying widths. This design is equally interesting when the rectangles are positioned horizontally.

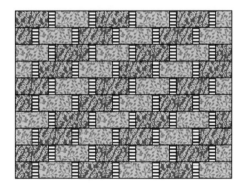

Horizontal arrangement

Try this design with two *contrasting* colors plus black-and-white stripes or a bold black-and-white print. You can alter the arrangement by substituting squares of black-and-white stripes for the rectangles and varying the placement of the squares.

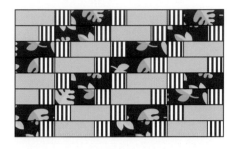

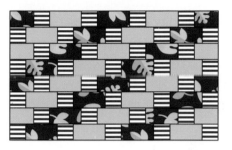

As you can see, these are just some of the variations that can be achieved simply by using two color families with added contrasts. All of these exercises in color, pattern, and value can also be applied to traditional block designs.

TRADITIONAL BLOCK DESIGN APPLICATIONS

WHEN BLOCKS are made up of only a few fabrics and repeated over the entire surface of the quilt, they can become boring to look at and boring to sew. Therefore, the greater the diversity of fabrics used in the blocks, the more interesting the surface design will be. The simplest block can be made more interesting by substituting different fabrics within the block.

Imagine you want to make a blue-and-yellow quilt using Nine Patch blocks. Traditionally, you would choose a light, medium, and dark fabric for the block (see A in photo on page 20).

Substitute one of the patches in each of the three fabrics with a patch that has similar values but a different print scale. Already there is a lot more to look at in the block (see B in photo below).

Keeping within the same value range, substitute other yellows and dark blues so that all the yellows and blues are different prints (see C in photo below).

The variation in the scale and pattern of the prints has created a much more interesting block, still within the format of the original. You can further substitute by changing the value of the patches. Substitute a yellow patch of darker value and a dark blue patch of lighter value. The lightest blue can be changed to a lighter or darker value. Now that the rigidity of the light, medium, and dark values has been altered, the eye is drawn to the dark yellow patch. Introduce a large, splashy print with other colors in it, and now there are two points of interest (see D in photo below).

Substitution can be taken a step further. Substitute a related color to the yellow and to the blue. Include a random patch of cool yellow (yellow with a green tinge). Violet is related to blue so occasionally substitute a violet patch. Introduce another large-scale yellow print that has another color in it (see E in photo below).

You can also introduce a random patch here and there of a completely different color for surprise value. Vary the blocks when making the quilt. Combine *all*

of the types of blocks shown (A–E), and see how the variations of color, pattern, and value transform the humble Nine Patch block into something special.

Variety of Nine Patch blocks with substituted patches

This method of selecting fabrics was used when designing "Pink Fizz" (page 45), "Secret Garden" (page 54), and "Square Dance" (page 90).

Here are more block variations for you to try. Play with different value arrangements. Many variations are possible. Each of these blocks can be split, and double and triple split for further complexity (refer to "Building Up the Design" on page 34).

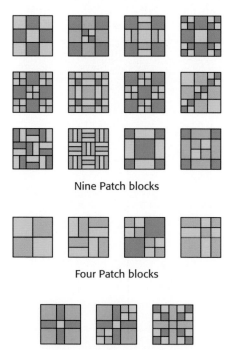

Nine Patch blocks

Four Patch blocks

Five Patch blocks

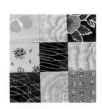

A   B

C   D   E

ASYMMETRICAL BLOCK DESIGNS

SUBDIVIDING a square into smaller squares and rectangles can create even more designs. For example, draw a 12" square on graph paper. Divide the square into smaller squares and rectangles.

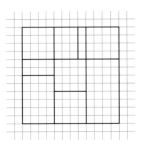

Asymmetrical block 1

Choose a large-scale print and related colors, varying the values and prints. Add two black-and-white prints for sparkle.

Asymmetrical block 1

The block can be further divided and additional related colors added, each in a different print.

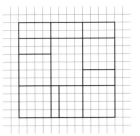

Asymmetrical block 2

Asymmetrical block 2

Use these blocks as the center of a quilt or cushion (see "Combo" on page 90), or combine them with other asymmetrical blocks in a unique quilt. Design more blocks, varying the size of the blocks, and experiment further with different color combinations.

6" block   8" block   10" block

14" block

Design ideas for asymmetrical blocks

LINKING LOGS:
LOG CABIN BLOCKS

*L*OG CABIN QUILTS have an enduring popularity because the block itself is so versatile. Traditionally, the Log Cabin block is made from strips of scrap fabrics (the logs) in a variety of light and dark colors. The strips are arranged so that half of the block is light and half of the block is dark. Originally, the center square was red to symbolize the chimney, but the size of the block, the center square, and the width of the logs can vary.

Variety of Log Cabin blocks

While the block description above doesn't seem to indicate anything special, this popular block can achieve dynamic results in a quilt because of the variety of ways the light and dark halves can be arranged to create different designs. Commonly set by themselves into such favorite quilt designs as Straight Furrow and Barn Raising, it's easy to add intricacy to a quilt design by splitting the blocks (see "Building Up the Design" on page 34) and adding sashing strips and joining squares (see "All That Jazz" on page 61 and "Razzle Dazzle" on page 91).

Value contrast is essential in scrap Log Cabin blocks, particularly when the blocks are set without sashing strips between the blocks. Unless there is a definite division of the block into light and dark halves, the design simply doesn't work. On the other hand, Log Cabin blocks that have strong contrast can be very stark. If all the light fabrics are very light and all the dark fabrics are very dark, it's a good idea to add some medium values to both groups. Just as you experimented with substitutions in Nine Patch blocks (see "Square Dance: Working with Squares and Rectangles" on page 15), occasionally substituting mediums for lights and darks in Log Cabin blocks will soften stark light and dark divisions in the block. Mediums act as a bridge between the two extremes and will therefore blend in with both value groups, adding interest to the blocks and stopping them from being predictable. Varying the scale of the prints will also add an extra dimension to the blocks. The use of large-scale prints blurs the regularity of the piecing and helps create focal points in the overall design.

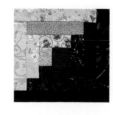
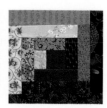

A   B   C

The same principle can be applied to blocks that are constructed from just one color family (monochromatic color scheme).

 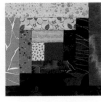 

| A | B | C |

Remember: variety is vital. Too much of the same color, the same print, the same scale of pattern, and the same value can become monotonous. You need to add some surprises (see "Crossroads" on page 91).

CONTROLLED LOG CABIN BLOCKS

THERE ARE some variations in Log Cabin blocks where the light and dark arrangement can be more controlled by limiting the number of fabrics used in the block and organizing their placement in a definite pattern.

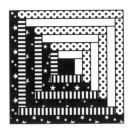

Block design with controlled
value arrangement

Choose the fabrics very carefully if you are limiting the color, pattern, and value range so that the quilt does not become boring. This means using a

| A | B | C |

wide variety of fabrics and either mixing the fabrics throughout the blocks or making sets of identical blocks.

The same type of block shown in the photo (below left) was used in "Daintree" (page 70). To achieve the variety of color and pattern I wanted and also control the arrangement in each block, I made eight sets of six identical blocks each. Then the blocks were grouped and enlarged with sashing strips between the blocks (see "Building Up the Design" on page 34) and arranged in diagonal rows. If you make blocks in sets, it is easier to calculate how much fabric you will need and it also simplifies the cutting and piecing of the units.

CENTER-SQUARE VARIATIONS

THE CENTERS of the blocks can be varied to give added interest to the overall design. The center square can be the same width as the logs, or it can be larger or smaller. It can also be pieced from half-square and quarter-square triangles (see "Crossroads" on page 91 and "Stripes 'n Stars" on page 92) or pieced in a four-patch or nine-patch unit.

Center square variations

While red is traditionally chosen for the center square, other colors work equally well (see "All That Jazz" on page 61). If you want to stay with red, try a print for a change or use a number of different reds in the same quilt. Using a variety of colors also works well (see "Currawongs" on page 92).

ACHIEVING CONTRAST

To ACHIEVE the contrast that is needed to make Log Cabin designs work well, you are not limited to using only light and dark arrangements. All that really matters is that the block is visually divided into two triangles with a diagonal axis. *Contrast* is the key point to consider. Color contrast and print contrast can be equally effective.

Color contrast defines the blocks in "Summer Citrus" (page 65). Although there is some value difference between the two colors (any fabric will be lighter or darker depending on the fabric placed next to it), the effect is achieved by dividing the block into yellow and orange. Some of the yellows are light and some are darker; the same holds true for the orange fabrics. Because each set of blocks has a different combination of fabrics, enough variety is achieved in terms of pattern contrast throughout the quilt. All fabrics vary in their value; when the focus shifts from value to color in the design, there is less emphasis on foreground and background areas. Sometimes the background becomes the foreground and vice versa.

The pieced center square in "Summer Citrus" (page 65) is important in helping the eye read the pattern. The black triangle faces the orange, which suggests "dark," and the pink triangle is aligned with the "light" yellow.

Compare "Summer Citrus" with "Razzle Dazzle" (page 91). Here many different colors and patterns are used in the blocks for "Razzle Dazzle," which again are constructed in sets of four. Note the variety and contrast in the prints and the use of solid colors. The yellow-and-black pieced center squares contrast vividly with the other fabrics that range from light to dark and bright to subdued. However, most of the fabrics are in the middle value range where colors are strongest, and therefore there are no foreground and background areas. The design is carried simply on the contrast between the two colors in each block.

Another way to achieve contrast is with the fabric print. "All That Jazz" (page 61) combines solids or tone-on-tone prints with stripes of varying widths. Because some of the stripes have white backgrounds, they are lighter than the solids. However, this does not apply to all the stripes, and there is still sufficient contrast in the blocks. The stripes set up a rhythm in the design that also contrasts with the solid blocks of color. If all the blocks were stripes or all the blocks were solids, you would not achieve the same rhythmic quality in the design.

You can also achieve contrast within one color family by contrasting the fabric prints and values (see "Soul Music" on page 88). In this quilt, the blocks are made up of blue prints that range from light to dark. There are many different blues, different types of prints, and different sizes of prints. There are medium values mixed with the lights and darks. There are also big splashy prints that have touches of other colors in them to add interest.

"Floral Trellis" (page 87) contrasts color, value, and print within two color families—red and yellow. The yellows in this quilt are not intense in their brightness, whereas the red is brighter, stronger, and more dominant than the yellow. Within the yellows and the reds, there is a range of values that also emphasizes foreground and background areas. Both color families include a variety of patterns, from small-scale patchwork prints to large-scale decorator fabrics.

As you can see, there are many starting points when selecting fabrics for a Log Cabin quilt. Think "contrast" and you can't go wrong. Once you've decided which approach to take, refer to "Piecing the Block" on page 26 to make up four blocks and play with them on the design wall. Start by arranging the blocks in traditional arrangements. To these arrangements, add single-, double-, or triple-split sashing strips (see "Building Up the Design" on page 34) until the desired result is achieved.

Traditional Log Cabin block arrangements in 4-block sets

The same Log Cabin blocks in 16-block sets

PIECING THE BLOCK

THE LOG Cabin block is built by adding logs around a center square in a clockwise or counterclockwise direction. Usually a light-colored fabric log is sewn to one side of the center square followed by another light log, which is placed perpendicular to the center square and first strip. Then a dark-colored fabric log is sewn to the third side of the unit, followed by another "dark" log. The second and subsequent rows repeat the order of the first row—two "lights" and two "darks." There is no rule that says you must start with light fabrics; you can begin with darks if you wish. The block can be pieced with the logs on the top of the square or underneath the square, whichever is more comfortable for you. The important thing is to be consistent so that the blocks are all the same.

Always make a block plan to determine the finished size of the block, the type of center square, and the width of the logs. The log width will be the same for all of the strips within a block. The log length is determined by the size of the center square and the logs that are attached to it. It is especially necessary to make a block plan if the center square is pieced and the logs must align a specific way (see "Summer Citrus" on page 65). Draft the finished block size on graph paper and number each log in the order it is to be attached to the center square; then add seam allowances to the center square and each log before rotary cutting the pieces.

Cut the logs to the correct size before you start piecing the blocks. This way, regardless of which direction you sew, you can't go wrong and the pieces will fit together and the blocks will all be the same size. Layer and cut the strips the required width; then stack them. The number of layers depends on the size and sharpness of the blade on your rotary cutter. The number of strips you crosscut depends on the number of blocks you are making from the same fabric.

It helps to organize the order of cutting and piecing so you can save time by chain-piecing (see "Machine Piecing" on page 8 for more information about chain-piecing). Start with a center square and a strip labeled #1. Chain-piece this unit with all the

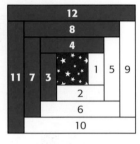

Clockwise

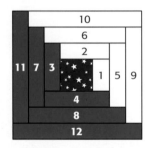

Counterclockwise

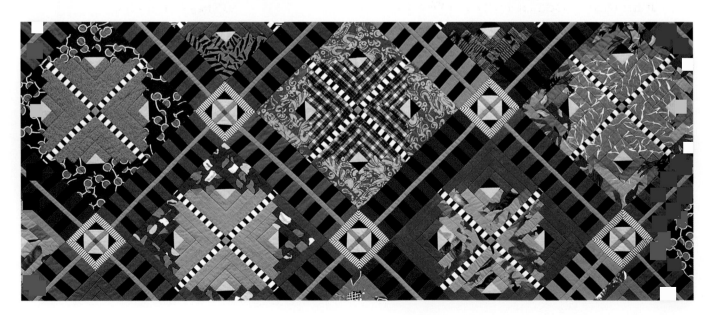

other center squares and strip #1 units; then go back and chain-piece the #2 strips to each unit. Continue chain piecing until the blocks are pieced.

RELATED BLOCKS

As you become more familiar with the Log Cabin block, you may want to try your hand at designing with other members of the Log Cabin family. In Courthouse Steps, the logs are pieced on opposite sides of the center square rather than around it (see "Crossroads" on page 91 and "Phoenix" on page 93). "Daintree" (page 70) shows the logs pieced to just two sides of the square. Other variations for you to try are shown below.

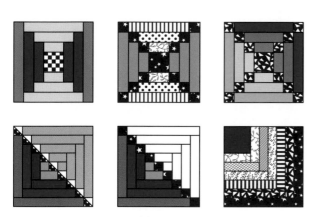

Related Log Cabin blocks

Further related blocks are the Ocean Waves/Log Cabin variation and the Nine Patch block, which has been split (see "Building Up the Design" on page 34). These blocks follow the same principle as the traditional Log Cabin block: a square divided into two triangles on a diagonal axis with a square in the center of the block. However, the pieces are not sewn around the center square. The Ocean Waves/Log Cabin variation is pieced in four triangular units. "Floral Trellis" (page 87) and "Soul Music" (page 88) show how the Ocean Waves/Log Cabin block looks when split. The split Nine Patch block is pieced in squares and joined together in rows.

Log Cabin variations

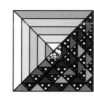

Ocean Waves variations

Split Nine Patch variations

All of these blocks look different when split, double split, triple split (see "Building Up the Design" on page 34), set straight, or set on point. Combined with the number of other setting variations, the design possibilities are endless.

I LOVE CRAZY piecing because it's a simple method for using many fabrics and achieves a very complex look. Any fabric can be used, even those frowned upon by the patchwork police, such as polyester and rayon! If the fabric is for a bed quilt, make sure it's washable; if the fabric is for a wall quilt that will never see a laundry tub, use any kind of fabric!

I have a large collection of fabric, accumulated over many years, and in that time I've made hundreds of quilts. Because I experiment on a design wall with strips and pieces of various colors and patterns until I find the "right" combination, the unused experimental fabric collects on the floor but is never, ever thrown away! Add to these the leftover strips, bindings, and trimmings from all the quilts I've ever made, and I have a lot of scraps. The scraps are stored in stackable plastic baskets in color families. I find these scraps to be extremely useful, particularly when experimenting and searching for the right color combination and especially for use in Crazy patchwork. I once made a quilt using red and yellow scraps, thinking that they would all be used up. To my surprise, the scrap baskets seemed almost as full when I finished as they did when I started. Do fabrics multiply in the dark when no one is around?

There are three approaches I take when "going Crazy":

- **Uncontrolled Crazy.** Use any color and fabric print.

- **Saturated Crazy.** Use one color and aim for richness, depth of color, and texture with a variety of fabrics.

- **Controlled Crazy.** Select fabrics from one color family, plus a contrast, a black and white, and a neutral. Combine the selections into definite light, medium, and dark arrangements.

All my Crazy piecing is sewn onto a foundation of muslin. Remember that the finished quilt will have an extra layer of fabric, and it will be heavier than your usual quilt top. A lightweight batting and backing, or just a backing fabric, is all you need.

Crazy blocks have lots of potential, whether set straight, split, double split, or sashed (refer to "Building Up the Design" on page 34). They are exciting to work with and provide an interesting juxtaposition to pieced sashing and borders.

FOUNDATION PREPARATION

1. Wash the foundation fabric thoroughly in warm water and detergent to eliminate the sizing and to allow for shrinkage. Add fabric softener to the final rinse. Repeat, if necessary, until the fabric is soft and wrinkle-free when pressed. Trim away the selvages.

    NOTE: *If you are making a wall hanging with fabrics that will never be laundered, there is no need to launder the foundation fabric.*

2. Determine the size of the finished block. If you are working mainly from your scrap basket, the size of the block will depend on what your scraps are like. If your scraps are large or your fabrics are bold and bright, try a 6" to 8" finished block. If the scraps are short lengths or small prints, sew a smaller, 4" to 6" finished-block size.

3. I like to Crazy piece onto a large foundation square and then cut the square into smaller squares. To do this, resize the foundation square to yield multiple blocks. Start by adding ½" for the seam allowance to the finished block size. For example, if the desired size of the finished block is 6", you would need a block that is 6½" square. Multiply this number by 2, and add 1" for a safety margin to make a foundation block that will yield 4 blocks when cut in half lengthwise and widthwise. For example, to cut 4 squares—each with a finished block size of 6"—from a larger square, you would need to piece a 14" block (6½" x 2 = 13" + 1" = 14").

Any foundation square *larger* than 16" becomes unworkable. (A 16" square would yield 4 squares, each with a finished size of 7".) To cut blocks with a finished size larger than 7", Crazy piece onto a foundation rectangle rather than a square, which will yield 2 squares. Add the seam allowance and 1" safety margin to the width and length of the rectangle, but only multiply one side by 2. For example, for an 8" finished block, you would cut a rectangle 9½" wide and 18" long (8½" + 1" = 9½" wide and 8½" x 2 = 17" + 1" = 18" long).

PIECING THE BLOCK

Uncontrolled Crazy

1. **Prepare the fabrics.** Sort your scraps and check the length of the pieces. The strips must extend beyond the edges of the foundation square or rectangle when placed at an angle across it. The strips should extend enough to cover the edge of the foundation square after they are stitched, flipped over, and pressed. In general, use long pieces for square foundations and short pieces for rectangular foundations.

Big, bold, and bright fabrics are great. Remember that *variety* is the most important factor in creating an interesting surface. Combine spots, stripes, plaids, checks, florals, tone-on-tones, solids, any "uglies" that you have never been able to use anywhere else, and any old pieces that have been lurking at the bottom of your stash for years. Unless you have a large collection of scraps, you will need to supplement from your stash. Don't get carried away with trying to match fabrics. Select purely on variety and contrast. Any polyester, rayon, or lightweight cotton fabrics will be stabilized by the foundation.

Once you've assembled your collection, press the fabrics. Set aside any strips that have already been cut to regular widths. These will be added to the wedge-shaped pieces you will cut next.

2. **Cut wedge-shaped pieces.** Just as it's important to have variety and contrast in your fabric selection, it's also important to have variety and contrast in the width and shape of the strips you cut. I like to use a wedge shape that is cut template-free with the rotary cutter and ruler. Wedge shapes help create an interesting and varied pieced block, more so than regular-width strips. Combining the two is fine, but include more wedge shapes than straight strips.

The size and width of these wedge shapes depends on the number of fabrics you're using. If you have a lot of different fabrics, it's exciting to cut each one only once. Avoid too much repetition of a fabric; it limits the options you have when arranging the blocks. Cut the wedges a variety of widths but no smaller than 1" wide at one end and no larger than 6" wide at the opposite end. Remember, they must extend beyond the edge of the foundation when placed at an angle. Don't worry about grain line too much; the wedges will be stabilized when stitched to the foundation fabric.

3. **Construct the block.** Select a wide strip and place it at an angle, right side up, across the center of the foundation block, from edge to edge. Hold it in place with a pin. Choose another strip of a contrasting size, color, and pattern; don't worry about whether they go together. Place it right side down on the first strip, matching right-hand raw edges. Using a ¼" seam allowance, stitch along the right-hand edge. Flip the fabric over, and finger-press the seam flat.

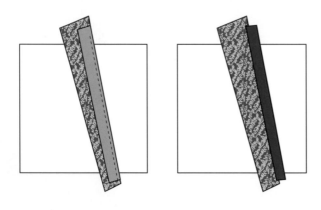

Turn the square around and repeat this process, stitching a second strip to the opposite edge of the first strip in the same manner.

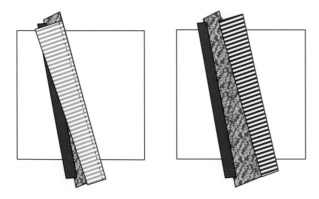

Press before adding more strips. Pressing is very important to ensure that the seams lie flat and do not bubble or ripple. I always work on more than one block so I can press as many seams at one time as possible. Repeat the process until the foundation is covered; press.

Do not make the squares the same. Angle the strips so that you create an interesting arrangement. Avoid an angle that is too oblique or too straight.

4. **Trim and recut the block.** Turn the square over, and neaten one edge with the rotary cutter and ruler. Turn the square a quarter turn, line up the cut edge with the top of the ruler, and neaten the second edge. Repeat with the remaining 2 sides.

Align the ruler with the 90° angle, and cut the foundation square into 2 strips the width of the desired block with seam allowances added. For example, if the finished block size is 6", cut a 6½" strip. Crosscut the strips to make 4 squares the desired size.

5. **Play with the block arrangement.** Once you have a stack of blocks completed, put them up on the design wall and experiment with different settings. This is always exciting, as there are lots of variations to try. Refer to "Rainbow Crazy" on page 93 and "Crazy Rhythm" on page 94 for inspiration.

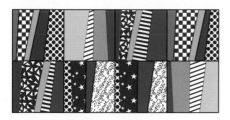

Straight set

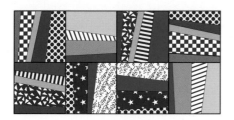

Basket weave

On point

Saturated Crazy

When you're aiming for a richness and density of color, Crazy patchwork with just one color family is very effective. Again, there is more than one approach you can take. Choose a color family such as red. Remember that the red color family extends to either side of the pure color. On a scale of light to dark, light reds (pinks) are at the light end of the scale and dark reds (burgundies) are at the other end of the scale. Pure color falls somewhere near the middle of the scale. The range shouldn't be limited to yellow-reds or blue-reds. Select any fabric that you recognize as red. Aim for variety in hue and contrast of pattern. Assemble your fabrics in a rough order

from light to dark. If the fabrics look good together on the table, they will also look good together when they are cut and pieced. If any fabric is glaringly out of place, remove it. Be adventurous. If you are not absolutely certain about that hot pink, leave it in. You may just love it in the finished block.

Assemble the Crazy blocks following the directions in "Uncontrolled Crazy" on page 29. The following photos will give you ideas for using color.

Option One

Use the entire range of your chosen color family, which will give you areas of strong light and dark contrast.

Option Two

Divide the color range in half and use only the range from light to medium, or use only the range from medium to dark. The light and dark contrast will be subtler.

Option Three

Divide the color range so that only lights, mediums, or darks are used.

For the most saturated, intense effect, choose fabrics from the middle range of the color family. Remember: this is where the color is purest and strongest (see "Sunshine and Flowers" on page 78 and "Force Field" on page 86). When you've assembled your fabrics, lay them out or stack them in a pile. Squint your eyes or look through a reducing glass. (A reducing glass works like a peephole in a door, reducing the image in front of you and allowing you to view the entire object as if it is at a distance.) If the fabrics are all very much alike in value, you're on the right track. If one is glaringly out of place, remove it. See "Building Up the Design" on page 34 for ideas for single-, double-, and triple-split blocks.

Controlled Crazy

Much of the attractiveness of Uncontrolled Crazy blocks and Saturated Crazy blocks is the result of accidental juxtaposition of color and pattern. Controlled Crazy blocks are another variation that offer even more design possibilities. Again, choose fabrics from one color family, but this time add a contrast and neutrals.

1. **Select the main color family.** Look for variety and contrast in pattern and color and, this time, in value—light, medium, and dark. Squint your eyes and compare the 3 piles. If a fabric is noticeably out of place in one pile, move it to another. There should be a definite separation of the 3 groups. To help you, make sure you add some very dark darks to the dark pile and some very light lights to the light pile. The mediums then generally take care of themselves.

2. **Choose the neutrals to be used with the main color.** These fabrics will not dominate, so you won't need as many as the main color, but you will need to sort them into light, medium, and dark as you did before for the main color. Select neutrals from the black, white, and gray range or the brown and beige range, whichever you prefer. Lay out the range. Make sure you have variety and contrast. When you are satisfied with the range, add the lights to the main-color light pile, the mediums with the main-color medium pile, and the darks with the main-color dark pile.

3. **Add the contrasting color fabrics.** Fabric from the contrasting color family can be anywhere on the scale of light to dark. You don't need many fabrics but, like the neutral, you need variety and contrast within this color family. Lay out your fabrics. The contrast color will be most effective if used in small amounts and should therefore be cut into narrow wedges and used sparingly. Cut some wedges and some narrow strips from your contrast group.

4. **Construct the blocks.** Refer to the instructions earlier in this chapter for block sizes and construction techniques. Begin with the light fabrics. Don't swamp your main color with too many neutrals. Include two or three wedges of

the contrast color, which can be light, medium, dark, or all three. Light contrast will blend into the other lights. Medium or dark contrast will stand out against the lights.

Follow the same procedure to make a block from the medium fabrics and another from the dark fabrics.

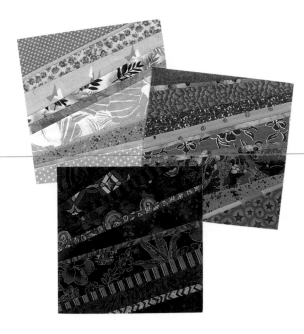

5. **Arrange the squares on the design wall.** Step back and check the value. Is there a definite difference between the light, medium, and dark blocks? If not, you probably need to add more dark darks and light lights to your groups. Check the effect of the contrast color. If the contrast color is too strong, continue the other blocks with a lighter contrast fabric.

All Crazy blocks can be used in a number of settings, sorted from light to dark, and may also be split and double split. See the following section, "Building Up the Design," for set ideas.

MOST OF THE quilts in this book are based on traditional blocks or are adaptations of traditional blocks. I've discussed in previous chapters how these blocks can be given extra dimension when constructed from many varieties of printed fabrics. A further dimension can be achieved by making the blocks appear more complex with the addition of sashing strips and sashing joining squares. These are called "split" blocks. The basic idea behind splitting the blocks is to build up the complexity of the design in easily constructed components. Sashing strips and sashing joining squares are just more squares and rectangles added to the blocks. The three types of split blocks—single, double, and triple—will be explained later in this chapter.

Changing the colors or prints of the fabrics can also vary each component, which adds another element to the design. Using striped fabrics for the sashing strips also can add to the complex appearance of the quilt. Stripes look like pieced work, and because of their graphic quality, they also add sparkle to the overall design. Adding sashing strips is not difficult, although using stripes for sashing strips and piecing the stripes takes a little more care; we will discuss that later in this chapter. If you join striped fabric with pieced sashing, you will also have an eye-catching combination. See how this combination is a good focal point in "All That Jazz" (page 61) and "Crossroads" (page 91).

The important point when making a quilt with sashing strips is that you must *sew a consistent seam allowance.* If you have ever made a group quilt, you will know that everyone sews a different ¼" seam! Therefore, ensure perfect piecing by measuring your pieced work and adjusting the measurements of the sashing strips if necessary.

SINGLE-SPLIT BLOCKS

There are two methods for constructing single-split blocks. The first method is to add sashing within the confines of the block design. For examples, let's look first at Four Patch and Nine Patch blocks. Both of these blocks can be split apart vertically and horizontally between the elements that make up the blocks. In these instances, the elements are the squares. Splitting the block apart between each element and adding a sashing strip not only enlarges it but gives it more complexity.

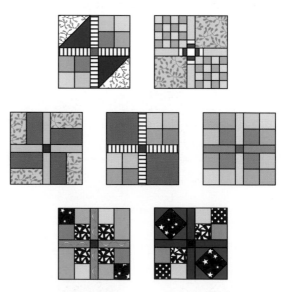

Four Patch blocks with sashing strips and joining square

The width of the sashing strips depends on the overall size of the block. Small blocks look better with narrow sashing strips, while larger blocks can have wider sashing strips. Blocks may be split with or without joining squares. Refer to the illustrations below and on page 34 for additional ideas for Four Patch and Nine Patch split blocks.

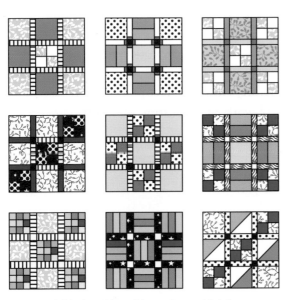

Nine Patch blocks with sashing strips and joining squares

Now, let's look at blocks with diagonal seams within the block, such as the Log Cabin and Ocean Wave variations shown on page 27. The same methods used for Four Patch and Nine Patch blocks applies to these blocks, but the sashing strips are cut longer than the sides of the triangles and trimmed when the block is completed. For an example of sashing strips added to a block with diagonal seams, see "Floral Trellis" on page 87.

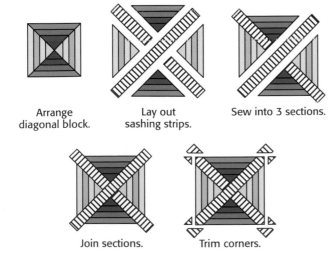

Arrange diagonal block.   Lay out sashing strips.   Sew into 3 sections.

Join sections.   Trim corners.

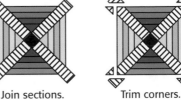

Arrange diagonal block.   Lay out sashing strips and joining square.   Sew into 3 sections.

Join sections.   Trim corners.

The second method of splitting the blocks is to group four blocks together and then split them with sashing to make a larger block.

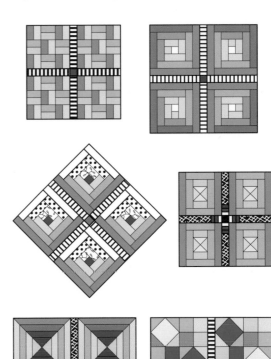
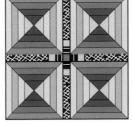
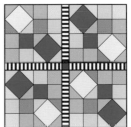

Sets of 4 blocks with added sashing strips and joining square

DOUBLE-SPLIT BLOCKS

ONCE THE blocks have been split, they can be grouped together in sets of four blocks and split again. Depending on the design of the block, some double-split blocks can be rotated to form secondary designs. Examples of quilts that use double-split blocks include "Rosella Maze" (page 49), "Secret Garden" (page 54), "All That Jazz" (page 61), and "Razzle Dazzle" (page 91).

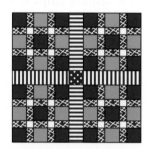

Double-split Four Patch   Double-split Nine Patch

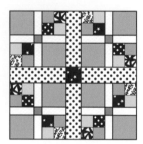

Rotated double-split blocks

Double splitting the blocks is yet another opportunity to introduce variations in color and print choices; it adds to the complex look. A simple way of achieving this is to vary the fabrics used in the sashing strips of those blocks that are set diagonally opposite each other (see "All That Jazz" on page 61, "Floral Trellis" on page 87, and "Crossroads" on page 91).

TRIPLE-SPLIT BLOCKS

DOUBLE-SPLIT blocks can be arranged in groups of four blocks and split again to make triple-split blocks. Look at "Secret Garden" (page 54), "Floral

Trellis" (page 87), "Soul Music" (page 88), and "Amethyst Windows" (page 94). In all of these quilts the fabrics have been varied in the opposing diagonal blocks. You can see how these variations add to the intricacy of the design. Triple-split sashing can be treated quite simply as in "Amethyst Windows" (page 94), or it can be another intricate element in the design by piecing the sashing and joining square as in "Secret Garden" (page 54) and "Soul Music" (page 88).

Triple-split set of Four Patch blocks

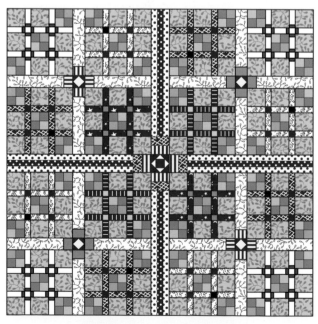

Triple-split set of Nine Patch blocks

JOINING SQUARES

JOINING SQUARES, both within the split blocks and separating the sashing strips, are an important focal point in any design. In their simplest form, they will create rhythm in the design when one fabric is used throughout (see "Composition in Red, Yellow, and Blue" on page 87) or when many values of one color are used (see "Square Dance" on page 90).

Pieced joining squares, such as those in "Stripes 'n Stars" on page 00, add an extra dimension to the design and are worth the extra effort. More intricately pieced joining squares add enormously to the eye-catching detail in a quilt, as you can see in "Razzle Dazzle" on page 91 and "Crazy Rhythm" on page 94.

PIECING STRIPED FABRICS

STRIPED FABRICS are usually printed with the stripes running parallel with the selvages. When cutting stripes, cut across the width of the fabric. To make sure the stripes are not cut crooked, align the horizontal markings on your ruler with the lines of the stripes. It will be necessary to straighten the cut edge from time to time.

It is not always possible when cutting stripes for block sashing strips to have the strips all exactly the same, especially in a Nine Patch block; a lot depends on the width of the stripe. Take time to look at how the stripe can best be cut for your project. Where possible, cut the pieces exactly the same, and plan where your seam allowance will be in relation to the width of the stripe. Be sure when a striped piece joins with a center square that the width of the first stripe on all the sashing strips is the same. It is very noticeable if they are not identical.

Designs for center squares and joining squares

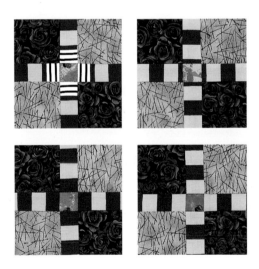

Not all of the stripes on a piece of fabric will be of equal width. If your fabric combines different widths within the one design, you may need extra fabric to create identical pieces. However, variegated striped fabrics can also be very useful because they can yield totally different patterns depending on where they are cut.

Stripes can also be cut from checks and plaids. Remember to take into account the width of your seam allowance when cutting.

Broaden your selection of stripes by cutting from checks and plaids.

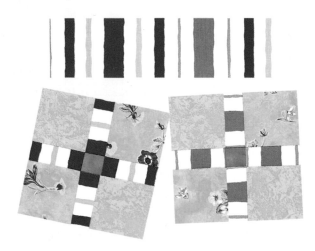

The same fabric can yield very different stripes.

When cutting and joining strips of striped fabric, always cut with the stripe. And unlike with print or solid fabrics, do *not* cut or join the strips at a 45° angle. Join two pieces together, stitching along the edge of the stripe—not down the middle of the stripe. The seam will then be unnoticeable. Press the seam open to reduce bulk.

NOTE: *When piecing stripes, always stitch the seam with the wrong side of the striped fabric on top. This way you can sew precisely with relation to the stripe.*

ESIGNING A QUILT doesn't stop once the quilt top is stitched together. Questions such as whether or not to add a border, what backing should be used, and how wide to cut the binding strips to effectively frame the quilt still need to be answered. This chapter will give you the basics for choosing the elements that will make your quilt a standout. For basics on how to add borders, assemble the layers, and bind the quilt, consult with a good basic quilting book, such as *The Joy of Quilting* (That Patchwork Place, 1994).

ADDING BORDERS

NOT ALL quilts need borders, yet others look better with a border added. How do you decide whether to add a border or not? Pin your quilt top to the design wall, and look at the overall design. If it seems unfinished and it needs framing, the top probably needs a border. Of course, if you're making a quilt for a bed and it's not quite large enough, you'll want to add a border for practical reasons. If you have used a lot of color and a variety of prints and split blocks in your quilt, there will be a lot of busyness in the quilt. A complicated pieced border would not enhance the design. If you're in doubt, audition different fabrics. Cut strips the finished border width, or fold the fabrics to the desired width, and pin them next to the quilt. Experiment with different prints and colors, multiple widths, and values. Some quilts look best with a simple narrow border; others will require a wide border, consisting perhaps of three or four strips of varying widths. If the border is too wide, it may look as though you didn't want to make any more blocks, so be careful of borders that are not in proportion to the other elements of your design. Be careful also that your border fabrics are not too dark as this will create a heavy frame around your work. The borders should frame the design and enhance it; therefore, the colors and prints used should complement the pieced work.

If nothing seems to work to your satisfaction, consider not having a border. Sometimes the design looks complete, and a carefully chosen binding is all that is needed. Have a look at the quilts in this book, and see the difference between the quilts with borders and those without. Sometimes, deciding whether to have a border and choosing the right fabrics for the borders and binding takes me almost as long as piecing the blocks, but it's always worth the extra effort.

CHOOSING THE BACKING FABRIC

ATTENTION TO detail makes the difference between an ordinary quilt and an extraordinary one. Choosing a backing fabric for your quilt shouldn't be an afterthought. Don't ruin an exciting design with a cheap and uncoordinated fabric on the back of the quilt. The color, pattern, and quality of the backing fabric should relate to the overall design and color of the patchwork.

If you can't find that one special fabric, consider piecing the backing from fabrics leftover from the quilt top. This can be challenging and fun. You can also piece any trial blocks into the backing to add to the total look of the quilt.

ATTACHING A HANGING SLEEVE

HANGING SLEEVES are a must for any quilt that will be hung. Be sure they are neat, hemmed, and unobtrusive. I suggest attaching the hanging sleeve to the quilt before binding so the raw edge can be enveloped when the quilt is bound.

SELECTING THE BINDING

CHOOSING THE correct binding should be given as much consideration as the selection of all the other fabrics. You cannot choose a binding fabric before the quilt top is completed and you can see the total design. The binding frames the design, and the color and pattern of the binding fabric should complement the colors and patterns in the quilt. If possible, pin your quilt top to the design wall and audition a number of fabrics. Cut narrow strips of fabric in the desired width, and pin them along the edge of the

quilt. The width of the binding may vary. A wide binding will be a little like another border and will be noticed (see "All That Jazz" on page 61 and "Square Dance" on page 90). Narrow bindings are more unobtrusive (see "Crossroads" on page 91). When the design does not need that extra frame, make the binding blend with the quilt by matching it to the main fabric or color in the quilt (see "Summer Citrus" on page 65), or piece it from printed fabrics used in the quilt (see "Sandy's Syncopation" on page 86 and "Secrets of the Bush" on page 89).

In general, for a ½"-wide finished binding, cut the fabric 3" wide. For a slightly narrower binding, cut the strips 2½" wide.

SIGNING OFF

THE QUILT is pieced, quilted, and bound, but it's not finished until you label it. If you don't have time to make hand-embroidered labels, use a good-quality laundry marker. Match the colors of the label to the backing fabric, or create a label from printed fabrics that relate to the colors in the quilt. Choose a title for your quilt and include it on the label, along with your name, the date, and any care instructions that are necessary. Sew the label to the quilt, and you are finished!

QUILT PROJECTS

FROG COURT

FROG COURT by Judy Hooworth, 1999, Sydney, Australia, 32½" x 40½" (85.5 cm x 107 cm).

• • •

Cool and warm colors contrast in this simple arrangement of split Four Patch blocks.

FINISHED BLOCK SIZE: *7" x 7" (18.5 cm x 18.5 cm)*
DESIGN: *Double-split Four Patch blocks*

MATERIALS

42"-wide fabric

- ½ yd. *total* of assorted violet, green, and blue solids for blocks
- ⅜ yd. *total* of assorted scraps of black-and-white, red, orange, blue, and yellow prints for single-split sashing strips and single-split sashing joining squares
- ½ yd. blue check for double-split sashing strips and inner borders
- 3½" x 5¼" rectangle of orange print for double-split sashing joining squares
- ⅛ yd. pink print for middle border
- ½ yd. violet-and-yellow print for outer border
- 37" x 45" piece of batting
- 1½ yds. fabric for backing
- ½ yd. green print for binding

CUTTING INSTRUCTIONS

All measurements include ¼" seam allowances.

From the violet, green, and blue solids, cut a *total* of:

- 48 squares, each 3½" x 3½", for blocks

From the assorted scraps of black-and-white, red, orange, blue, and yellow prints, cut a *total* of:

- 12 squares, each 1½" x 1½", for single-split sashing joining squares
- 12 rectangles, each 3½" x 6". Crosscut into 4 strips, each 1½" x 3½", for single-split sashing strips.

From the blue check, cut:

- 4 strips, each 1¾" x 42". Crosscut into 17

rectangles, each 1¾" x 7½", for double-split sashing strips.

- 2 strips, each 2" x 24", for inner top and bottom borders
- 2 strips, each 2" x 35¼", for inner side borders

From the orange print, cut:

- 2 strips, each 1¾" x 5¼". Crosscut into 6 squares, each 1¾" x 1¾", for double-split sashing joining squares.

From the pink print, cut:

- 2 strips, each 1" x 27", for middle top and bottom borders
- 2 strips, each 1" x 36¼", for middle side borders

From the violet-and-yellow print, cut:

- 2 strips, each 3" x 28", for outer top and bottom borders
- 2 strips, each 3" x 41¼", for outer side borders

From the green print, cut:

- 4 strips, each 3" x 42", for binding

QUILT TOP ASSEMBLY

1. Using 4 assorted 3½" solid-color squares, 4 identical 1½" x 3½" sashing strips, and 1½" x 1½" sashing joining square, assemble each block as shown. Press the seam allowances toward the rectangles. Make 12.

Make 12.

2. To make the block rows, alternately stitch together 3 blocks and two 1¾" x 7½" sashing strips, beginning and ending with a block. Press the seam allowances toward the sashing strips. Make 4 rows.

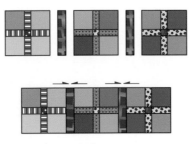

Make 4.

3. To make the sashing rows, alternately stitch together three 1¾" x 7½" sashing strips and two 1¾" x 1¾" sashing joining squares, beginning and ending with a sashing strip. Press the seam allowances toward the sashing strips. Make 3 rows.

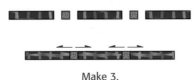

Make 3.

4. Beginning and ending with a block row, stitch the block and sashing rows together. Press the seam allowances toward the sashing rows.

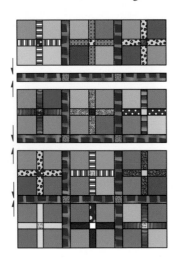

5. Stitch the inner top and bottom borders to the top and bottom edges of the quilt. Press the seam allowances toward the borders. Stitch the inner side borders to the quilt sides. Press the seam allowances toward the borders. Repeat for the center and outer border strips.

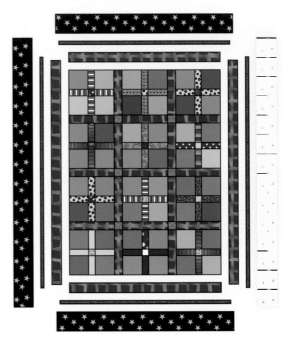

QUILT FINISHING

1. Layer the quilt top with batting and backing; baste.

2. Quilt as desired.

3. Trim the batting and backing even with the quilt top.

4. Bind the quilt with the green strips.

5. Stitch a label to the quilt back.

PINK FIZZ

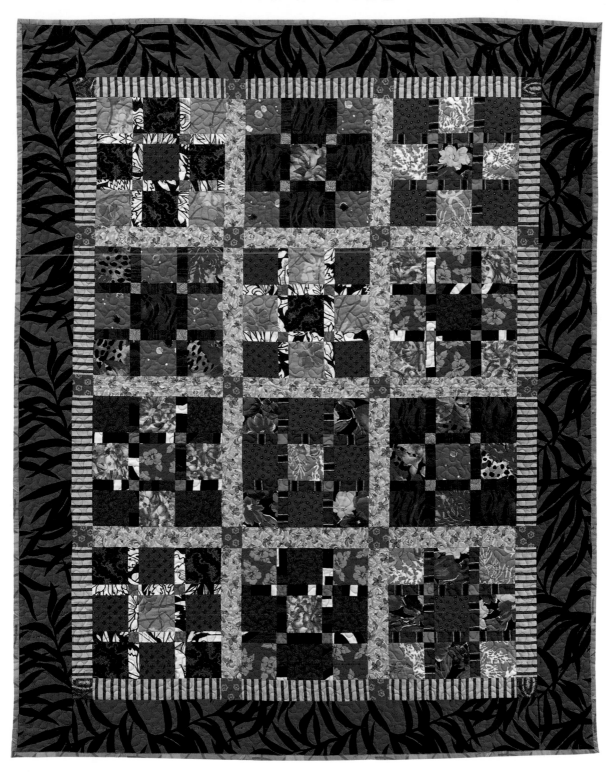

PINK FIZZ by Judy Hooworth, 1999, Sydney, Australia, 58" x 72½" (146.5 cm x 184.5 cm). Quilted by Kerry Adams.

· · ·

A bold pink-and-black border print contrasts with the bright yellow-print sashing
that frames the double-split Nine Patch blocks.

FINISHED BLOCK SIZE: *12½" x 12½" (32 cm x 32 cm)*
DESIGN: *Double-split Nine Patch blocks*

MATERIALS

42"-wide fabric

- 12" x 12" square *each* of 12 assorted pink prints for blocks
- ¼ yd. *each* of 4 assorted violet prints for single-split sashing strips
- 3" x 9" rectangle *each* of 4 assorted blue prints for single-split sashing joining squares
- ½ yd. yellow print for double-split sashing strips
- ½ yd. yellow-and-black lengthwise-striped print for double-split sashing strips
- 10" x 10" square of pink print for double-split sashing joining squares
- 5" x 5" square of violet print for double-split sashing corner squares
- 1¼ yds. pink-and-black print for border
- 62" x 77" piece of batting
- 4 yds. fabric for backing
- ¾ yd. blue print for binding

CUTTING INSTRUCTIONS

All measurements include ¼" seam allowances.

From *each* of the 12" x 12" assorted pink squares, cut:

- 3 strips, each 4" x 12". Crosscut into 9 squares, each 4" x 4", for blocks.

From *each* of the assorted violet prints, cut:

- 4 strips, each 1½" x 42". Crosscut into 36 strips, each 1½" x 4", for single-split sashing strips.

From *each* of the 3" x 9" assorted blue rectangles, cut:

- 2 strips, each 1½" x 9". Crosscut into 12 squares, each 1½" x 1½", for single-split sashing joining squares.

From the yellow print, cut:

- 6 strips, each 2½" x 42". Crosscut into 17 strips, each 2½" x 13", for double-split sashing strips.

From the yellow-and-black striped print, cut:

- 5 strips, each 2½" x 42". Crosscut into 14 strips, each 2½" x 13", for double-split sashing strips.

From the 10" x 10" square of pink print, cut:

- 4 strips, each 2½" x 10". Crosscut into 16 squares, each 2½" x 2½", for double-split sashing joining squares.

From the 5" x 5" square of violet print, cut:

- 4 squares, each 2½" x 2½", for double-split sashing corner squares

From the pink-and-black print, cut:

- 6 strips, each 6½" x 42", for border

From the blue print, cut:

- 7 strips, each 3" x 42", for binding

QUILT TOP ASSEMBLY

1. Divide the pink 4" squares into 4 groups, keeping all of the squares cut from one print together. There should be 3 different fabrics in each group. Label the prints in *each* group as A, B,

and C. To each group, add 36 identical violet 1½" x 4" sashing strips, and 12 identical blue 1½" x 1½" joining squares. Each group makes up 1 set. Each set will yield 3 identical blocks.

2. Refer to the arrangement diagram to arrange 1 of each of the 3 block combinations from each set. Stitch the blocks together as shown. Press the seam allowances toward the sashing strips.

Arrangement of Group 1 fabrics

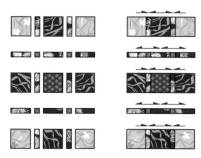

3. To make the block rows, alternately stitch together 3 blocks and 2 yellow-print 2½" x 13" sashing strips, beginning and ending with a block. Stitch a yellow-and-black, 2½" x 13" sashing strip to the ends of each row. Press the seam allowances toward the sashing strips. Make 4 rows.

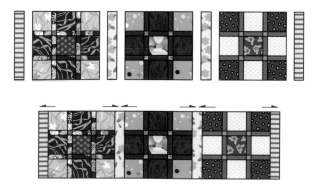

Make 4.

4. To make the sashing rows, alternately stitch together 4 pink-print 2½" x 2½" sashing joining squares and 3 yellow-print 2½" x 13" sashing

strips, beginning and ending with a joining square. Press the seam allowances toward the sashing strips. Make 3 rows.

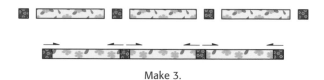

Make 3.

5. To make the top and bottom outer sashing rows, alternately stitch together 3 yellow-and-black 2½" x 13" sashing strips and 2 pink-print 2½" x 2½" sashing joining squares, beginning and ending with a sashing strip. Stitch a violet 2½" x 2½" sashing corner square to the ends of each row. Press the seam allowances toward the sashing strips. Make 2 rows.

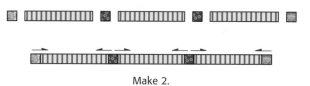

Make 2.

6. Beginning and ending with a block row, stitch the block and sashing rows together. Stitch the top and bottom outer sashing rows to the top and bottom edges. Press the seam allowances toward the sashing rows.

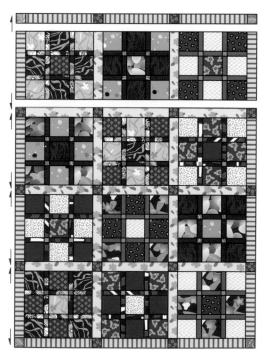

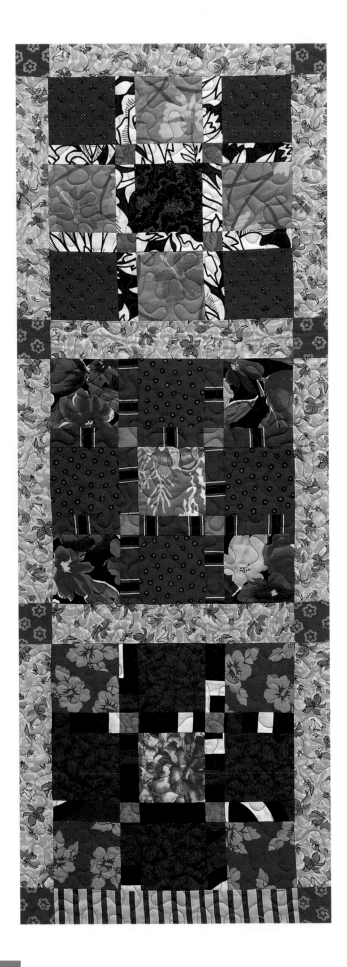

7. Stitch the pink-and-black border strips together into one long strip. From the strip, cut 2 segments, each 6½" x 46", for the top and bottom borders; and cut 2 strips, each 6½" x 72½", for the side borders. Stitch the top and bottom borders to the top and bottom edges of the quilt. Press the seam allowances toward the borders. Stitch the side borders to the quilt sides. Press the seam allowances toward the borders.

QUILT FINISHING

1. Cut the backing fabric in half widthwise and join the 2 pieces together lengthwise. Trim the backing to 62" x 77". Layer the quilt top with batting and backing; baste.

2. Quilt as desired.

3. Trim the batting and backing even with the quilt top.

4. Bind the quilt with the blue-print strips.

5. Stitch a label to the quilt back.

ROSELLA MAZE

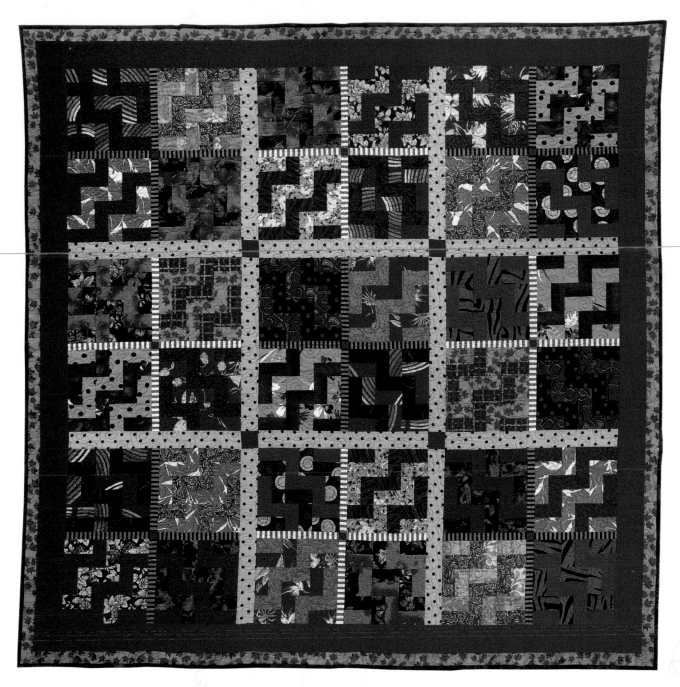

ROSELLA MAZE by Judy Hooworth, 2000, Sydney, Australia, 92½" x 92½" (232 cm x 232 cm). Quilted by Kerry Adams.

• • •

The traditional Rail Fence block is transformed with a vivid combination of red, blue, and yellow prints.

MATERIALS

42"-wide fabric

- ¼ yd. *each* of 18 assorted red prints for blocks
- ¼ yd. *each* of 9 assorted dark blue prints for blocks
- ¼ yd. *each* of 9 assorted light blue prints for blocks
- ½ yd. black-and-pink lengthwise-striped print for single-split sashing strips
- 3" x 4½" rectangle of pink print for single-split sashing joining squares
- ⅜ yd. blue-and-white, lengthwise-striped print for single-split sashing strips
- 3" x 3" square violet print for single-split sashing joining squares
- ⅞ yd. yellow-and-violet polka dot fabric for double-split sashing strips
- 6" x 6" square red print for double-split sashing joining squares
- 1⅜ yds. red-and-black, lengthwise-striped print for inner border
- ⅞ yd. blue print for outer border
- 96" x 96" square of batting
- 6¾ yds. fabric for backing
- ⅞ yd. dark blue print for binding

CUTTING INSTRUCTIONS

All measurements include ¼" seam allowances.

From *each* of the assorted dark blue and light blue fabrics, cut:

- 2 strips, each 2½" x 42", for blocks

From *each* of the assorted red fabrics, cut:

- 2 strips, each 2½" x 42", for blocks

From the black-and-pink striped print, cut:

- 7 strips, each 1½" x 42". Crosscut into 20 strips, each 1½" x 12½", for single-split sashing strips.

From the pink print, cut:

- 2 strips, each 1½" x 4½". Crosscut into 6 squares, each 1½" x 1½", for single-split sashing joining squares. Discard 1 square.

From the blue-and-white striped print, cut:

- 6 strips, each 1½" x 42". Crosscut into 16 strips, each 1½" x 12½", for single-split sashing strips.

From the violet print, cut:

- 4 squares, each 1½" x 1½", for single-split sashing joining squares

From the yellow-and-violet polka dot fabric, cut:

- 12 strips, each 3" x 25½", along the lengthwise grain for double-split sashing strips

From the 6" x 6" square of red print, cut:

- 4 squares, each 3" x 3", for double-split sashing joining squares

From the red-and-black striped print, cut:

- 9 strips, each 4½" x 42", for inner border

From the blue print, cut:

- 10 strips, each 2½" x 42", for outer border

From the dark blue print, cut:

- 9 strips, each 3" x 42", for binding

QUILT TOP ASSEMBLY

1. Stitch a red 2½" x 42" strip to a 2½" x 42" light blue strip to make a strip set. Press the seam allowance toward the blue fabric. Make 18 red-and-light-blue strip sets. Stitch a red 2½" x 42" strip to a 2½" x 42" dark blue strip to make a strip set. Press the seam allowance toward the blue fabric. Make 18 red-and-dark-blue strip sets. Cut each strip set into 9 segments, each 4½" x 4½", for a total of 18 segments with the same blue and red fabric combination.

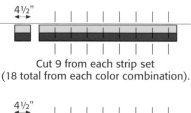

Cut 9 from each strip set
(18 total from each color combination).

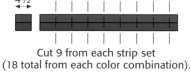

Cut 9 from each strip set
(18 total from each color combination).

2. Refer to the illustrations to stitch the segments into blocks as shown. Be careful to arrange the segments together exactly as shown. Press the seam allowances in one direction. Make 18 A blocks from the red-and-dark-blue segments and 18 B blocks from the red-and-light-blue segments.

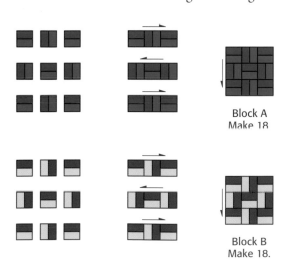

Block A
Make 18

Block B
Make 18.

3. To make the split blocks, stitch together 2 different A blocks, 2 different B blocks, 4 black-and-pink 1½" x 1½" sashing strips, and 1 pink 1½" x 1½" sashing joining square as shown. Pay close attention to the placement of each block. Match the stripe width and color where it joins the center square. Press the seam allowances toward the striped fabric pieces. Make 5.

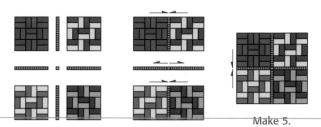

Make 5.

4. Repeat step 3 with the remaining blocks, the blue-and-white 1½" x 12½" sashing strips, and the violet 1½" x 1½" sashing joining squares. Make 4.

5. Pin the completed blocks to your design wall or lay them on the floor. Place the blocks with the black-and-pink sashing strips in the 4 corners and the quilt center. Fill in the spaces with the remaining blocks. Check the block placement. Make sure the dark blue fabrics create a diagonal line across the quilt from left to right, and the light blue fabrics create a diagonal line across the quilt from right to left.

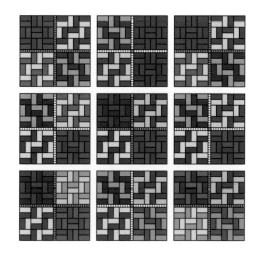

6. To make the block rows, keep the blocks in the same position as they were on the design wall and alternately stitch each horizontal row of 3

blocks together with 2 yellow-and-violet double-split sashing strips, beginning and ending with a block. Press the seam allowances toward the double-split sashing strips. Make 3 rows.

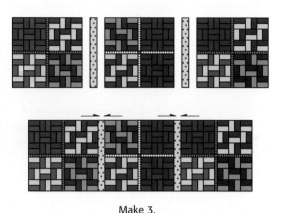

Make 3.

7. To make the double-split sashing rows, alternately stitch together 3 yellow-and-violet 3" x 25½" sashing strips and 2 red 3" x 3" sashing joining squares, beginning and ending with a sashing strip. Press the seam allowances toward the sashing strips. Make 2 rows.

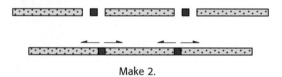

Make 2.

8. Beginning and ending with a block row, stitch the block and sashing rows together. Press the seam allowances toward the sashing rows.

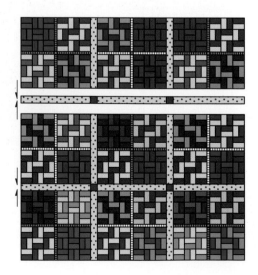

9. Stitch the red-and-black inner border strips together to make one long strip. From the strip, cut 2 segments, each 4½" x 80½", for the inner top and bottom borders; and cut 2 segments, each 4½" x 88½", for the inner side borders. Stitch the inner top and bottom borders to the top and bottom edges of the quilt. Press the seam allowances toward the borders. Stitch the inner side borders to the quilt sides. Press the seam allowances toward the borders. Stitch the blue-print outer border strips together to make one long strip. From the strip, cut 2 segments, each 2½" x 88½", for the outer top and bottom borders; and cut 2 segments, each 2½" x 92½", for the outer side borders. Stitch the outer top and bottom borders to the top and bottom edges of the quilt. Press the seam allowances toward the borders. Stitch the inner side borders to the quilt sides. Press the seam allowances toward the borders.

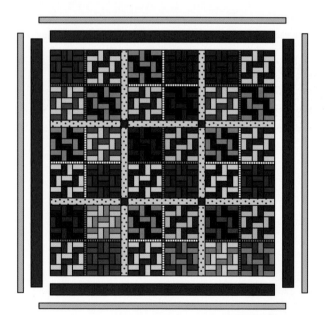

QUILT FINISHING

1. From the backing fabric, cut 2 pieces, each 42" x 96". Cut the remaining fabric in half lengthwise to yield 2 pieces, each 21" x 51". Stitch the 21"-long edges together to make 1 strip, 21" x 102". Stitch the 2 full-width pieces and the half-width piece together along the long edges. Trim the pieced backing to 96" x 96".

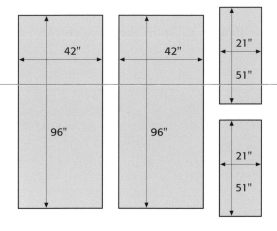

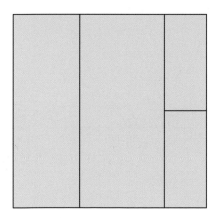

Trim to 96" x 96".

2. Layer the quilt top with batting and backing; baste.

3. Quilt as desired.

4. Trim the batting and backing even with the quilt top.

5. Bind the quilt with the dark blue strips.

6. Stitch a label to the quilt back.

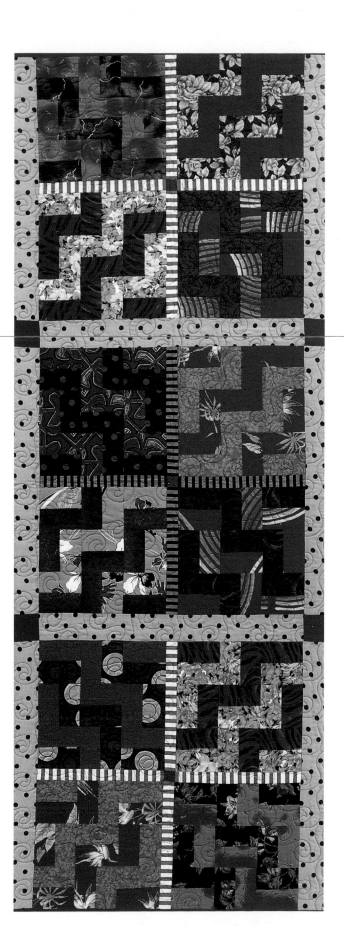

SECRET GARDEN

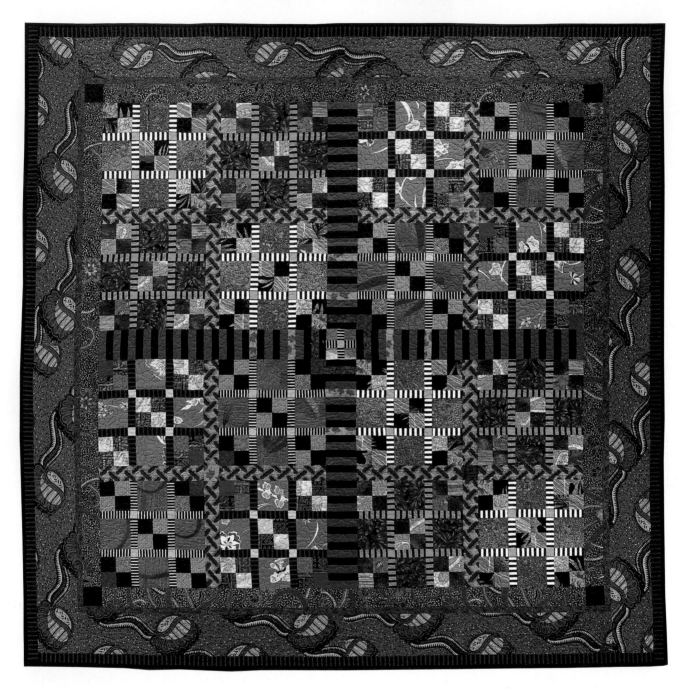

SECRET GARDEN by Judy Hooworth, 2000, Sydney, Australia, 84" x 84" (213 cm x 213 cm). Quilted by Kerry Adams.

• • •

Rich earthy shades in a wide variety of prints enhance these Nine Patch blocks in a triple-split set.

FINISHED BLOCK SIZE: 14" x 14" (35 cm x 35 cm)
DESIGN: Triple-split Nine Patch blocks

MATERIALS

42"-wide fabric

- ⅜ yd. *each* of 4 assorted brown floral prints for blocks
- ⅜ yd. *each* of 4 assorted black and dark violet prints for blocks
- ¼ yd. *each* of 4 assorted peach and apricot prints for blocks
- ⅛ yd. *each* of 4 assorted orange prints for blocks
- ⅛ yd *each* of 4 assorted light violet prints for blocks
- ½ yd. *each* of 4 assorted lengthwise-striped prints for single-split sashing strips and triple-split sashing joining square
- 6" x 6" square *each* of 4 assorted light blue solids for single-split sashing joining squares
- ¾ yd. violet-and-brown print for double-split sashing strips
- 2½" x 5" rectangle of violet-and-black print for double-split sashing joining squares
- 2½" x 5" rectangle of blue-and-black print for double-split sashing joining squares
- 1⅝ yds. black solid for triple-split sashing strips, first border corner squares, and binding
- ½ yd. brown solid for triple-split sashing strips
- ⅛ yd. blue print for triple-split sashing strips
- ⅛ yd. bright violet print for triple-split sashing strips
- 4" x 4" square orange print for triple-split sashing joining square
- 1½" x 1½" square light blue solid for triple-split sashing joining square
- ¾ yd. brown-and-black print for first border

- ⅜ yd. bright violet print for second border
- 1¾ yds. large floral print for third border
- ⅝ yd. red-and-black lengthwise-striped print for fourth border
- 89" x 89" square of batting
- 6¼ yds. fabric for backing

CUTTING INSTRUCTIONS

All measurements include ¼" seam allowances.

From *each* of the assorted brown floral prints, cut:
- 2 strips, each 4½" x 42". Crosscut into 16 squares, each 4½" x 4½", for blocks.

From *each* of the assorted black and dark violet prints, cut:
- 3 strips, each 2½" x 42", for blocks

From *each* of the assorted peach and apricot prints, cut:
- 2 strips, each 2½" x 42", for blocks

From *each* of the assorted orange prints and light violet prints, cut:
- 1 strip, 2½" x 42", for blocks

From *each* of the assorted striped prints, cut:
- 9 strips, each 1½" x 42". Crosscut into 48 *identical* strips, each 1½" x 4½", for single-split sashing strips.

From the remainder of one of the assorted striped prints, cut:
- 4 *identical* strips, each 1½" x 2½", for triple-split sashing joining square

From *each* of the assorted light blue solids, cut:

- 4 strips, each 1½" x 6". Crosscut into 16 squares, each 1½" x 1½", for single-split sashing joining squares.

From the violet-and-brown print, cut:

- 8 strips, each 2½" x 42". Crosscut into 16 strips, each 2½" x 14½", for double-split sashing strips.

From *both* the violet-and-black print and the blue-and-black print, cut:

- 2 squares, each 2½" x 2½", for double-split sashing joining squares

From the black solid, cut:

- 7 strips, each 1½" x 42", for triple-split sashing strips
- 4 squares, each 2½ x 2½", for first border corner squares
- 9 strips, each 3" x 42", for binding

From the brown solid, cut:

- 7 strips, each 1½" x 42", for triple-split sashing strips

From *both* the blue print and bright violet print, cut:

- 1 strip, 1½" x 42", for triple-split sashing strips

From the 4" square of orange print, cut:

- 2 strips, each 2" x 4". Crosscut into 4 squares, each 2" x 2", for triple-split sashing joining square.

From the brown-and-black print, cut:

- 7 strips, each 2½" x 42", for first border

From the bright violet print, cut:

- 7 strips, each 1½" x 42", for second border

From the large floral print, cut:

- 8 strips, each 6" x 42", for third border

From the red-and-black striped print, cut:

- 8 strips, each 2" x 42", for fourth border

QUILT TOP ASSEMBLY

1. Begin by placing the following pieces into 4 groups; all of the pieces from one print should be in the same group. Each group should have 16 brown floral 4½" squares; 3 black or dark violet, 2 peach or apricot, 1 orange, and 1 light violet 2½" x 42" strips; 48 striped-print 1½" x 4½" strips; and 16 light blue solid 1½" squares. Label the groups 1–4.

2. To make the blocks, begin with the pieces in group 1. Stitch each peach or apricot strip to a black or dark violet strip to make a strip set. Make 2 strip sets. Press the seam allowances toward the black or dark violet strips. From the strip sets, cut a total of 24 segments, each 2½".

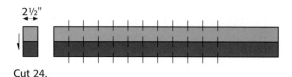

Cut 24.

3. Stitch 2 segments together as shown to make a Four Patch block. Make 12.

Make 12.

4. Cut each orange strip, light violet strip, and remaining black or dark violet strip into 2 strips, each 2½" x 21". Discard 1 orange and 1 light violet strip. Stitch the remaining orange strip to a black or dark violet strip, and stitch the light violet strip to the remaining black or dark violet strip. From each strip set, cut 8 segments, each 2½" wide.

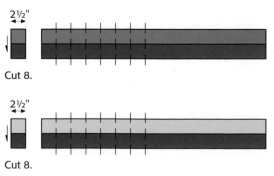

Cut 8.

Cut 8.

5. Stitch each orange-and-dark segment from step 4 to a violet-and-dark segment as shown. Make 8 Four Patch blocks.

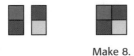

Make 8.

6. Using the Four Patch blocks from steps 3 and 4 and the remaining pieces in group 1, refer to the single-split arrangement diagram to arrange each single-split block. Stitch the pieces together as shown. Press the seam allowances toward the striped-print strips. Make 4 *identical* blocks.

Dark black or purple print
Apricot or peach print
Orange print
Light violet print
Brown floral print
Light blue solid
Stripe

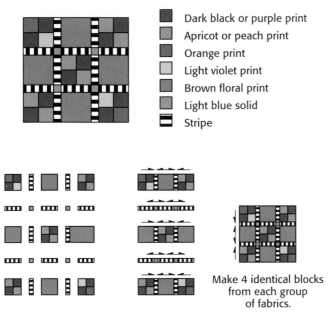

Make 4 identical blocks from each group of fabrics.

Single-split arrangement

7. Repeat steps 2–5 for groups 2, 3, and 4. Make sure the colors in each group of blocks are placed in exactly the same position as group 1.

8. To make the double-split blocks, combine groups 1 and 2 and combine groups 3 and 4. Refer to the double-split arrangement diagrams below and on next page. Arrange the blocks with the violet-and-brown 2½" x 14½" sashing strips and the violet-and-black or blue-and-black 2½" x 2½" sashing joining squares. Use the violet-and-black sashing joining squares with groups 1 and 2, and use the blue-and-black sashing joining squares with groups 3 and 4. Press the seam allowances toward the sashing strips. Make 2 double-split blocks with groups 1 and 2, and 2 double-split blocks with groups 3 and 4.

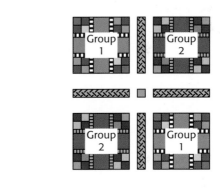

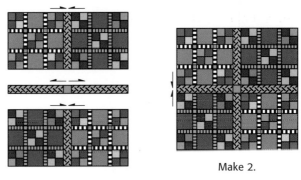

Make 2.

Double-split arrangement for groups 1 and 2

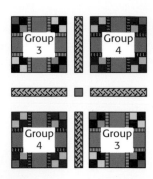

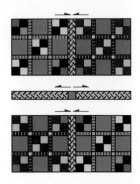
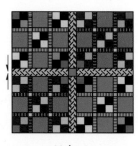

Double-split arrangement for groups 3 and 4

Make 2.

9. To make the triple-split strips, cut the black solid, brown solid, blue print, and bright violet triple-split sashing strips into 2 strips, each 1½" x 21". Discard 1 bright violet strip and 1 brown solid strip. Refer to the illustration to stitch the strips together into Strip Set 1. Reverse the direction each strip is sewn so the finished piece remains flat. Press the seams in one direction. Square up one end of the strip set; then cut Strip Set 1 into 4 segments, each 4½" wide.

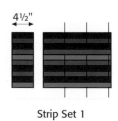

4½"

Strip Set 1

10. Use the remaining black solid and brown solid strips from step 8 to make Strip Set 2. Alternately stitch 20 strips together, starting with black and ending with brown. Square up one end of Strip Set 2; then cut the strip set into 4 segments, each 4½" wide.

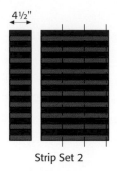

4½"

Strip Set 2

11. Stitch the black end of a segment from Strip Set 2 to the blue end of a segment from Strip Set 1. Make 4.

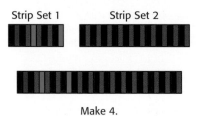

Strip Set 1   Strip Set 2

Make 4.

12. To make the sashing joining square, stitch the light blue 1½" square, the 4 orange 2" squares, and the 4 identical striped-fabric 1½" x 2½" strips together as shown.

13. Stitch the blocks, sashing strips, and sashing joining square together as shown. Press the seam allowances toward the blocks.

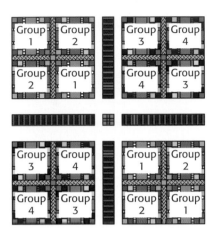

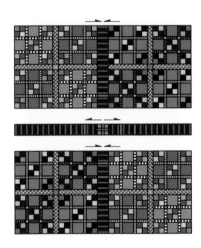

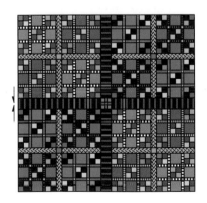

14. Stitch the first border strips together into one long strip. From the strip, cut 4 segments, each 2½" x 64½". Stitch a strip to the top and bottom edges of the quilt top. Stitch the 2½" black solid squares to the ends of the remaining strips. Stitch the pieced border strips to the quilt sides. Press the seam allowances toward the border strips.

15. Stitch the second border strips together to make one long strip. From the strip, cut 2 segments, each 1¼" x 68½", for the second top and bottom borders; and cut 2 segments, each 1¼" x 70", for the second side borders. Stitch the second top and bottom borders to the top and bottom edges of the quilt top. Stitch the second side borders to the quilt sides. Press the seam allowances toward the border strips.

16. Stitch the third border strips together to make one long strip. From the strip, cut 2 segments, each 6" x 70", for the third top and bottom borders; and cut 2 segments, each 6" x 81", for the third side borders. Stitch the third top and bottom borders to the top and bottom edges of the quilt top. Stitch the third side borders to the quilt sides. Press the seam allowances toward the border strips.

17. Stitch the fourth border strips together to make one long strip. From the strip, cut 2 segments, each 2" x 81", for the fourth top and bottom borders; and cut 2 segments, each 2" x 84", for the fourth side borders. Stitch the fourth top and bottom borders to the top and bottom edges of the quilt top. Stitch the fourth side borders to the quilt sides. Press the seam allowances toward the border strips.

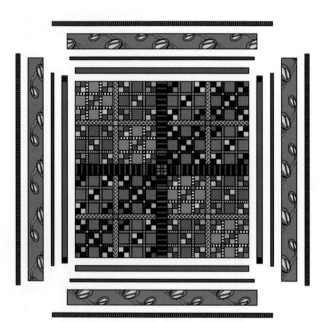

QUILT FINISHING

1. Cut the backing fabric into 2 pieces, each 42" x 89". Cut the remaining fabric in half lengthwise, and stitch the ends together to make 1 long piece. Stitch the 3 pieces together lengthwise, and trim to 89" x 89".

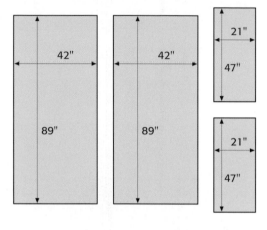

Trim to 89" x 89".

2. Layer the quilt top with batting and the pieced backing; baste.

3. Quilt as desired.

4. Trim the batting and backing even with the quilt top.

5. Bind the quilt with the black solid strips.

6. Stitch a label to the quilt back.

ALL THAT JAZZ

ALL THAT JAZZ by Judy Hooworth, 2000, Sydney, Australia, 70½" x 70½" (178 cm x 178 cm). Quilted by Kerry Adams.

• • •

Brights and stripes reverberate in this colorful arrangement of double-split Log Cabin blocks.

FINISHED BLOCK SIZE: 10" x 10" (25 cm x 25 cm)
DESIGN: Double-split Log Cabin blocks

MATERIALS

42"-wide fabric

- ¼ yd. *each* of 18 assorted solids or tone-on-tone prints for blocks
- ¼ yd. *each* of 18 assorted lengthwise-striped prints for blocks
- ½ yd. black-and-white print for block center squares and double-split sashing joining squares
- ½ yd. dark black-and-white lengthwise-striped print (A) for single-split sashing strips
- ½ yd. light black-and-white lengthwise-striped print (B) for single-split sashing strips
- 4" x 6" rectangle of red solid for single-split sashing joining squares
- 4" x 4" square of blue solid for single-split sashing joining square
- ⅞ yd. violet solid or tone-on-tone print for double-split sashing strips and binding
- ¼ yd. black-and-white striped print for double-split sashing strips
- ¾ yd. yellow solid for double-split sashing strips
- 4¼ yds. fabric for backing
- 75" x 75" square of batting

CUTTING INSTRUCTIONS

All measurements include ¼" seam allowances.

From *each* of the 18 assorted solid or tone-on-tone prints, cut:

- 3 strips, each 1½" x 42", for blocks. Crosscut and label the strips as follows:

    2 strips, each 1½" x 3½"; label #3

    2 strips, each 1½" x 4½"; label #4
    2 strips, each 1½" x 5½"; label #7
    2 strips, each 1½" x 6½"; label #8
    2 strips, each 1½" x 7½"; label #11
    2 strips, each 1½" x 8½"; label #12
    2 strips, each 1½" x 9½"; label #15
    2 strips, each 1½" x 10½"; label #16

From *each* of the 18 assorted striped prints, cut:

- 3 strips, each 1½" x 42", for blocks. Crosscut and label the strips as follows:

    2 strips, each 1½" x 2½"; label #1
    2 strips, each 1½" x 3½"; label #2
    2 strips, each 1½" x 4½"; label #5
    2 strips, each 1½" x 5½"; label #6
    2 strips, each 1½" x 6½"; label #9
    2 strips, each 1½" x 7½"; label #10
    2 strips, each 1½" x 8½"; label #13
    2 strips, each 1½" x 9½"; label #14

From the black-and-white print, cut:

- 3 strips, each 2½" x 42". Crosscut into 36 squares, each 2½" x 2½", for block center squares.
- 4 squares, each 3½" x 3½", for double-split sashing joining squares

From the dark black-and-white striped print (A), cut:

- 7 strips, each 2" x 42". Crosscut into 20 strips, each 2" x 10½", for single-split sashing strips.

From the light black-and-white striped print (B), cut:

- 6 strips, each 2" x 42". Crosscut into 16 strips, each 2" x 10½", for single-split sashing strips.

From the 4" x 6" red solid rectangle, cut:

- 3 strips, each 2" x 6". Crosscut into 6 squares, each 2" x 2", for single-split sashing joining squares.

From the 4" x 4" blue solid square, cut:

- 2 strips, each 2" x 4". Crosscut into 4 squares, each 2" x 2", for single-split sashing joining squares.

From the violet solid or tone-on-tone print, cut:

- 2 strips, each 1½" x 42", for double-split sashing strips
- 7 strips, each 3" x 42", for binding

From the black-and-white striped print for double-split sashing strips, cut:

- 2 strips, each 1½" x 42"

From the yellow solid, cut:

- 6 strips, each 3½" x 42". Crosscut into:
    8 strips, each 3½" x 20", for double-split sashing strips
    4 strips, each 3½" x 18", for double-split sashing strips

QUILT TOP ASSEMBLY

1. Pair a set of solid 1½" strips (#3, 4, 7, 8, 11, 12, 15, and 16) with a set of striped 1½" strips (#1, 2, 5, 6, 9, 10, 13, and 14). From the pairs, make 2 identical groups, integrating the striped and solid strips so they are in numerical order. Place the #16 strip on the bottom and the #1 strip on the top of the stacks. Place a black-and-white print 2½" square on the top of each stack. Repeat with the remaining 17 solid and striped strip sets. When finished, you will have 18 sets of 2 identical strip groups.

2. To make each block, take an integrated strip stack and sew piece #1 to a 2½" center square. Press the seam allowance away from the center. Add piece #2 to the top of the center square and #1 unit. Press the seam allowance away from the

center. Continue adding strips counterclockwise in numerical order around the center square. Make a total of 36 blocks.

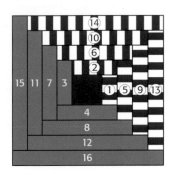

3. Stitch together 2 sets of identical blocks, 4 dark black-and-white (A) 2" x 10½" sashing strips, and 1 red 2" x 2" sashing joining square as shown. Press the seam allowances toward the sashing strips. Make 5. Repeat with the remaining blocks, with light black-and-white (B) 2" x 10½" sashing strips, and blue 2" x 2" sashing joining squares. Make 4.

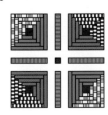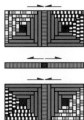

Make 9 total.

4. Stitch a violet or tone-on-tone double-split sashing strip to a black-and-white double-split sashing strip. Press the seam allowance toward the striped strip. Make 2. Crosscut the strips into 16 segments, each 3½" wide.

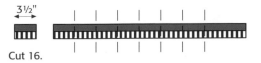

3½"

Cut 16.

5. Stitch a violet and black-and-white striped segment to each end of each 3½" x 18" yellow strip. Stitch a violet and black-and-white striped segment to one end of each 3½" x 20" yellow strip.

Make 4.   Make 8.

6. To make the top and bottom block rows, alternately stitch together 3 blocks and 2 sashing strips with a striped segment at one end as shown, beginning and ending with a block. Press the seam allowances toward the sashing strips. Refer to the illustration to position blocks with red sashing joining squares at each end of the rows. Make 2 rows.

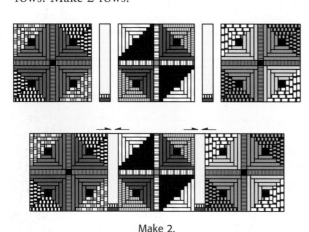

Make 2.

7. Repeat step 6 for the center block row, but use sashing strips with a striped segment at each end and place a block with a red sashing joining square in the center of the row.

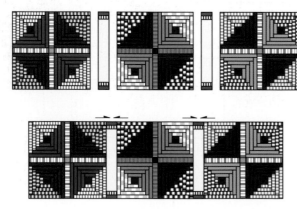

Make 1.

8. To make the double-split sashing rows, alternately stitch 3 sashing strips and 2 sashing joining squares together, beginning and ending with a sashing strip. Press the seam allowances toward the sashing strips. Make 2.

Make 2.

9. Stitch the block rows and sashing rows together. Press the seam allowances toward the sashing rows.

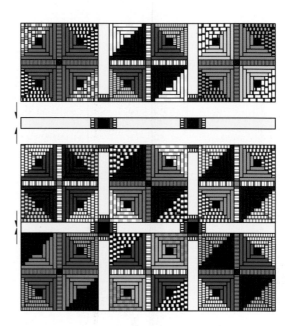

QUILT FINISHING

1. Cut the backing fabric in half widthwise. Stitch the 2 pieces together lengthwise. Trim the piece to 75" x 75".

2. Layer the quilt top with batting and the pieced backing; baste.

3. Quilt as desired.

4. Trim the batting and backing even with the quilt top.

5. Bind the quilt with the violet strips.

6. Stitch a label to the quilt back.

SUMMER CITRUS

SUMMER CITRUS by Judy Hooworth, 2000, 51" x 51" (128.5 cm x 128.5 cm). Quilted by Kerry Adams.

• • •

Warm summer orange and yellow prints make up these split Log Cabin blocks, which are set on point in this striking design.

MATERIALS

42"-wide fabric

- 8" x 10" rectangle of pink print for block center squares
- 8" x 10" rectangle of black solid for block center squares
- ¼ yd. *each* of 6 assorted yellow prints for blocks
- ¼ yd. *each* of 6 assorted orange prints for blocks
- ¼ yd. blue print for single-split sashing strips and single-split sashing joining squares
- ¼ yd. of black print for single-split and double-split sashing joining squares
- ¼ yd. black-and-white lengthwise-striped print for single-split sashing strips
- 1¼ yds. orange-and-yellow print for corner triangles, setting triangles, and binding
- ¾ yd. orange-and-black print for double-split sashing strips
- 55" x 55" square of batting
- 2¼ yds. fabric for backing

CUTTING INSTRUCTIONS

All measurements include ¼" seam allowances.

From *each* of the pink print and black solid rectangles, cut:

- 3 strips, each 2⅜" x 10". Crosscut into 12 squares, each 2⅜" x 2⅜". Cut each square in half diagonally to make 24 half-square triangles for blocks.

From *each* of the assorted yellow prints, cut:

- 3 strips, each 1½" x 42", for blocks. Crosscut and label the strips as follows:
    4 strips, each 1½" x 2"; label #1
    4 strips, each 1½" x 3"; label #2
    4 strips, each 1½" x 4"; label #5
    4 strips, each 1½" x 5"; label #6
    4 strips, each 1½" x 6"; label #9
    4 strips, each 1½" x 7"; label #10

From *each* of the assorted orange prints, cut:

- 4 strips, each 1½" x 42", for blocks. Crosscut and label the strips as follows:
    4 strips, each 1½" x 3"; label #3
    4 strips, each 1½" x 4"; label #4
    4 strips, each 1½" x 5"; label #7
    4 strips, each 1½" x 6"; label #8
    4 strips, each 1½" x 7"; label #11
    4 strips, each 1½" x 8"; label #12

From the blue print, cut:

- 4 strips, each 1½" x 42". Crosscut into:
    16 strips, each 1½" x 8", for single-split sashing strips
    5 squares, each 1½" x 1½", for single-split sashing joining squares

From the black print, cut:

- 1 strip, 2½" x 42". Crosscut into 12 squares, each 2½" x 2½", for double-split sashing joining squares.
- 4 squares, each 1½" x 1½", for single-split sashing joining squares

From the black-and-white striped print, cut:

- 3 strips, each 1½" x 42". Crosscut into 12 *identical* strips, each 1½" x 8", for single-split sashing strips.

From the orange-and-yellow print, cut:

- 2 squares, each 13¼" x 13¼". Cut the squares twice diagonally to make 8 quarter-square setting triangles.
- 2 squares, each 12¼" x 12¼". Cut each square in half diagonally to make 4 half-square corner triangles.
- 5 strips, each 2½" x 42", for binding

From the orange-and-black print, cut:

- 8 strips, each 2½" x 42". Crosscut into 16 strips, each 2½" x 16½", for double-split sashing strips.

QUILT TOP ASSEMBLY

1. Stitch a pink half-square triangle to a black solid half-square triangle to make the block center square. Make 24.

Make 24.

2. Pair each set of yellow 1½" strips (#1, 2, 5, 6, 9, and 10) with a set of orange 1½" strips (#3, 4, 7, 8, 11, and 12). From each pair, make 4 identical groups, integrating the yellow and orange strips so they are in numerical order. Place the #12 strip on the bottom and the #1 strip on the top of each stack. Place a pieced center square on the top of each integrated stack. Repeat with the remaining 5 yellow and orange strip sets. When finished, you will have 6 sets of 4 identical strip groups.

3. To make each Log Cabin block, sew piece #1 to the pink side of the pieced center square. Press the seam allowance away from the center. Add piece #2 to the top of the center square and piece #1 unit. Press the seam allowance away from the center. Continue adding strips counterclockwise in numerical order around the center square. Make a total of 24 blocks. Separate the blocks into 6 sets of 4 identical blocks.

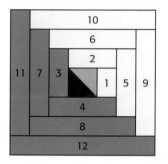

Make 6 sets of 4 identical blocks.

4. Stitch together 1 set of identical Log Cabin blocks, 4 blue 1½" x 8" sashing strips, and 1 black 1½" x 1½" sashing joining square as shown. Place the Log Cabin blocks so the orange half of each block is toward the center of the split block. Press the seam allowances toward the sashing strips. Make 4. In the same manner, stitch together 1 set of identical Log Cabin blocks, 4 black-and-white 1½" x 8" sashing strips, and 1 blue 1½" x 1½" sashing joining square. Make 1.

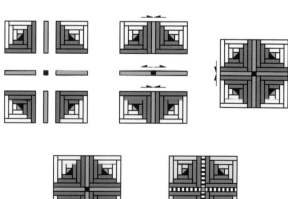

Make 4.   Make 1.

5. Stitch a black-and-white 1½" x 8" sashing strip to one orange side of each of the remaining Log Cabin blocks. Press the seam allowance toward the sashing strip. Stitch a blue 1½" x 1½" sashing joining square to one end of each of the remaining black-and-white strips. Press the seam allowance toward the sashing strip. Stitch the pieced strips to the remaining orange side of each Log Cabin block. Press the seam allowance toward the sashing strip.

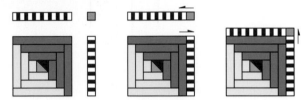

6. Stitch an orange-and-yellow quarter-square setting triangle to the striped sides of each block from step 5. Be sure to place the quarter-square setting triangles so the straight grain will be on the outside edge. Trim the blue sashing joining square even with the setting triangles. Press the seam allowances toward the striped sashing strips.

Trim.

7. To make the block rows, stitch together 1 block from step 4, 2 setting triangle units from step 6, and two 2½" x 16½" sashing strips as shown. Make 2.

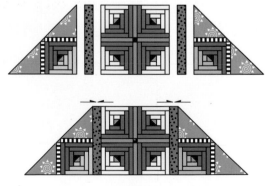

Make 2.

8. Stitch together the remaining 3 blocks from step 4 and four 2½" x 16½" sashing strips as shown. Make 1. Press the seam allowances toward the sashing strips.

Make 1.

9. To make the sashing rows, alternately stitch together four 2½" x 2½" sashing joining squares and three 2½" x 16½" sashing strips, beginning and ending with a sashing joining square. Make 2. In the same manner, alternately stitch together two 2½" x 2½" sashing joining squares and one 2½" x 16½" sashing strip. Make 2. Press the seam allowances toward the sashing strips.

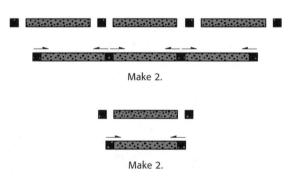

Make 2.

Make 2.

10. Assemble the block rows and sashing rows diagonally as shown. Stitch the rows together. Press the seam allowances toward the sashing rows.

11. Trim the sashing joining squares on the quilt outer edges even with the quarter-square setting triangles. Stitch an orange-and-yellow half-square corner triangle to each corner.

QUILT FINISHING

1. Cut a 54" length from the backing fabric. Cut the remaining backing fabric in half widthwise. Stitch the strips together end to end to make 1 long piece. Stitch the pieced strip to the side of the 54" length to make a 54" square.

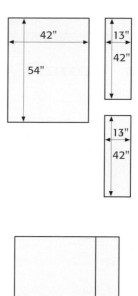

Trim to 54" x 54".

2. Layer the quilt top with batting and the pieced backing; baste.

3. Quilt as desired.

4. Trim the backing and batting even with the quilt top.

5. Bind the quilt with the orange-and-yellow strips.

6. Stitch a label to the quilt back.

DAINTREE

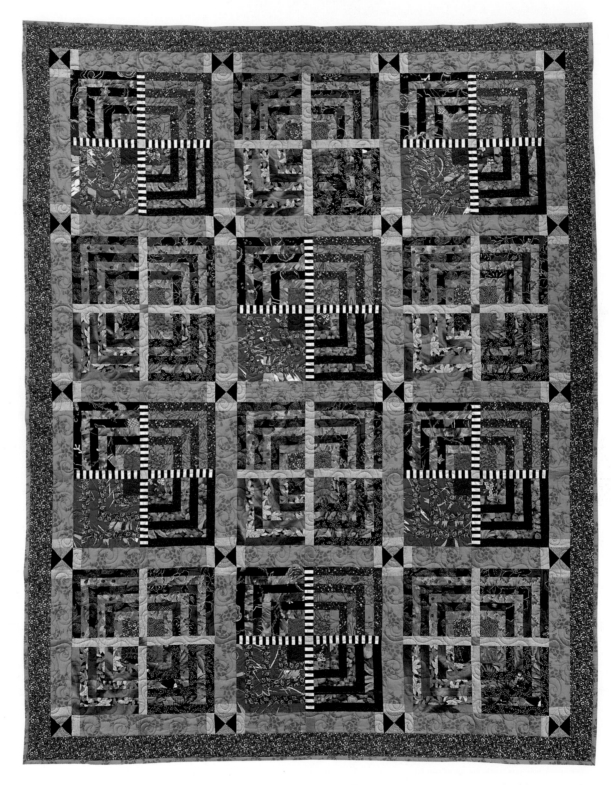

DAINTREE by Judy Hooworth, 2000, Sydney, Australia, 67" x 86½" (169.5 cm x 218.5 cm). Quilted by Kerry Adams.

• • •

A palette of cool colors enhances the double-split, off-sided Log Cabin blocks.

FINISHED BLOCK SIZE: 8"x 8" (20 cm x 20 cm)
DESIGN: Double-split, off-sided Log Cabin blocks

MATERIALS

42"-wide fabric

- ⅜ yd. *each* of 8 assorted green prints for blocks
- ⅜ yd. *each* of 4 assorted blue prints for blocks
- ⅜ yd. *each* of 4 assorted black prints for blocks
- 5" x 7½" rectangle *each* of 8 assorted violet prints for blocks
- ⅜ yd. black-and-white lengthwise-striped print for single-split sashing strips
- 3" x 4½" rectangle of yellow print for single-split sashing joining squares
- 3" x 4½" rectangle of blue print for single-split sashing joining squares
- ⅝ yd. chartreuse yellow print for single-split sashing strips and double-split sashing strips
- ¼ yd. black solid for double-split sashing joining squares
- ¼ yd. light blue print for double-split sashing joining squares
- ¼ yd. light violet solid for double-split sashing strips
- 2 yds. aqua print for double-split sashing strips and binding
- 1 yd. violet print for border
- 72" x 91" piece of batting
- 5⅛ yds. fabric for backing

CUTTING INSTRUCTIONS

All measurements include ¼" seam allowances.

From *each* of the assorted green prints, cut:

- 5 strips, each 1½" x 42", for blocks. Crosscut and label the strips as follows:

  6 strips, each 1½" x 2½"; label #1
  6 strips, each 1½" x 3½"; label #2
  6 strips, each 1½" x 4½"; label #5
  6 strips, each 1½" x 5½"; label #6
  6 strips, each 1½" x 6½"; label #9
  6 strips, each 1½" x 7½"; label #10

From *each* of the assorted blue prints and black prints, cut:

- 6 strips, each 1½" x 42", for blocks. Crosscut and label the strips as follows:

  6 strips, each 1½" x 3½"; label #3
  6 strips, each 1½" x 4½"; label #4
  6 strips, each 1½" x 5½"; label #7
  6 strips, each 1½" x 6½"; label #8
  6 strips, each 1½" x 7½"; label #11
  6 strips, each 1½" x 8½"; label #12

From *each* of the assorted violet-print rectangles, cut:

- 2 strips, each 2½" x 7½". Crosscut into 6 squares, each 2½" x 2½", for blocks.

From the black-and-white striped print, cut:

- 6 strips, each 1½" x 42". Crosscut into 24 *identical* strips, each 1½" x 8½", for single-split sashing strips.

From *both* the yellow-print rectangle and the blue-print rectangle, cut:

- 2 strips, each 1½" x 4½". Crosscut into 6 squares, each 1½" x 1½", for single-split sashing joining squares.

From the chartreuse yellow print, cut:

- 6 strips, each 1½" x 42". Crosscut into 24 strips, each 1½" x 8½", for single-split sashing strips.
- 5 strips, each 1½" x 42", for double-split sashing strips

From *both* the black solid and light blue print, cut:

- 1 strip, 3¾" x 42". Crosscut into 10 squares, each 3¾" x 3¾"; cut each square twice diagonally to make 40 quarter-square triangles for double-split sashing joining squares.

From the light violet solid, cut:

- 3 strips, each 1½" x 42", for double-split sashing strips

From the aqua print, cut:

- 5 strips, each 7½" x 42", for double-split sashing strips
- 8 strips, each 3" x 42", for binding

From the violet print for border, cut:

- 8 strips, each 3½" x 42"

QUILT TOP ASSEMBLY

1. Pair each set of green 1½" block strips (#1, 2, 5, 6, 9, and 10) with a set of blue or black 1½" strips (#3, 4, 7, 8, 11, and 12). From each pair, make 6 identical groups, integrating the green and blue or black strips so they are in numerical order. Place the #12 strip on the bottom and the #1 strip on the top of each stack. Place a violet 2½" square on the top of each integrated stack. Repeat with the remaining 7 green and blue or black strip sets. When finished, you will have 8 sets of 6 identical strip groups.

2. To make each block, sew piece #1 to the violet center square. Press the seam allowance away from the square. Add piece #2 to the bottom of the center square and piece #1 unit. Press the seam allowance away from the center. Continue adding strips in numerical order to the side and bottom of the center square. Make a total of 48 blocks.

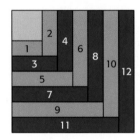

Make 48 total.

3. Separate the blocks into 8 sets of 6 identical blocks each. Divide the sets into 2 groups, placing 2 blue/green sets and 2 black/green sets in each group.

4. Using the blocks in the group 1 stack, stitch together 4 different blocks, 4 black-and-white 1½" x 8½" sashing strips, and 1 yellow 1½" x 1½" sashing joining square as shown. Press the seam allowances toward the sashing strips. Make 6 *identical* split blocks. Repeat with the blocks in group 2. Use the chartreuse yellow 1½" x 8½" sashing strips and blue 1½" x 1½" sashing joining squares. Make 6 *identical* split blocks.

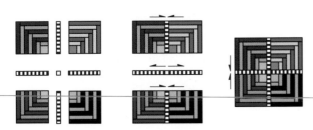

Make 6.   Make 6.

5. Stitch each black quarter-square triangle to a light blue quarter-square triangle. Be sure to place the quarter-square setting triangles so the straight grain will be on the outside edge. Stitch 2 pairs together as shown to make the sashing joining squares. Make 20.

Make 20.

6. Stitch 2 chartreuse yellow, 1 light violet, and 2 aqua double-split sashing strips together as shown to make a strip set. Press the seam allowances toward the aqua strips. Make 3. From the strip sets, cut a total of 31 segments, each 3" wide.

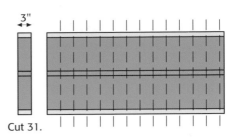

3"

Cut 31.

7. To make the block rows, alternately stitch together 2 blocks with black-and-white sashing strips, 1 block with chartreuse yellow sashing strips, and 4 pieced sashing strips from step 6 as shown. Press the seam allowances toward the sashing strips. Make 2 rows. Stitch together 2 blocks with chartreuse yellow sashing strips, 1 block with black-and-white sashing strips, and 4 pieced sashing strips from step 6 as shown. Make 2 rows.

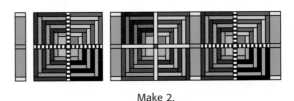

Make 2.

Make 2.

8. To make the sashing rows, alternately stitch together 4 pieced sashing joining squares from step 5 and 3 pieced sashing strips from step 6, beginning and ending with a joining square. Make 5 rows.

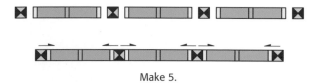

Make 5.

9. Alternately stitch together the block and sashing rows, beginning and ending with a sashing row.

10. Stitch the border strips together into one long strip. From the strip, cut 2 segments, each 3½" x 61½", for the top and bottom borders; and cut 2 strips, each 3½" x 87", for the side borders. Stitch the top and bottom borders to the top and bottom edges of the quilt. Press the seam allowances toward the borders. Stitch the side borders to the quilt sides. Press the seam allowances toward the borders.

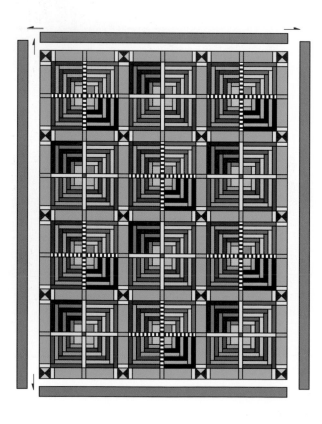

QUILT FINISHING

1. Cut the backing fabric into 2 pieces, each 42" x 91". Stitch the pieces together lengthwise. Trim to 72" x 91".

2. Layer the quilt top with batting and the pieced backing; baste.

3. Quilt as desired.

4. Trim the backing and batting even with the quilt top.

5. Bind the quilt with the aqua strips.

6. Stitch a label to the quilt back.

BLUE SWIMMERS

BLUE SWIMMERS by Judy Hooworth, 1998, Sydney, Australia, 52½" x 60" (133 cm x 152 cm).

• • •

The complementary colors of blue and orange are combined in a Controlled Crazy set.
Blue swimmer crabs are a Sydney seafood delicacy.

Finished Block Size: 7½" x 7½" (19 cm x 19 cm)
Design: Controlled Crazy

MATERIALS

42"-wide fabric

- Assortment of blue-print scraps at least 1½" x 11" in light, medium, and dark values for blocks*
- Assortment of black-, gray-, and white-print scraps at least 1½" x 11" in light, medium, and dark values for blocks*
- Assortment of orange-print scraps at least 1½" x 11" in light, medium, and dark values for blocks*
- 3½ yds. muslin for block foundations
- 55" x 64" piece of lightweight batting (optional)
- 3¼ yds. fabric for backing
- ½ yd. black print for binding

    *You should have approximately 1 yard *total* of light scraps, 1½ yards *total* of medium scraps, and 2 yards *total* of dark scraps.

CUTTING INSTRUCTIONS

All measurements include ¼"- seam allowances.

From the muslin for block foundations, cut:
- 7 strips, each 17" x 42". Crosscut to make 28 rectangles, each 9" x 17".

From the black print for binding, cut:
- 6 strips, each 3" x 42"

QUILT TOP ASSEMBLY

1. Combine the fabric scraps into 3 groups—1 each of lights, mediums, and darks.

2. Refer to "Going Crazy" on page 28 to review the instructions for Crazy piecing. Cut the light orange prints into wedges approximately ¾" to 2" wide and 11" long. Cut the remaining light value scraps into wedges approximately 1½" to 6" wide and 11" long. Stitch the wedges to 6 muslin foundation rectangles. Trim the rectangles and recut into 12 blocks, each 8" x 8".

3. Repeat step 2 with the medium-value prints. Make 9 rectangles. Trim and recut the rectangles into 18 blocks, each 8" x 8".

4. Repeat step 2 with the dark-value prints. Make 13 rectangles. Trim and recut the rectangles into 26 blocks, each 8" x 8".

5. Arrange the blocks, turning them as desired until you are pleased with the composition. Place the light, medium, and dark blocks as shown in the diagram.

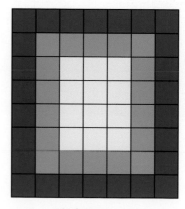

Block placement

6. Stitch the blocks together into 8 rows of 7 blocks each. Press the seams open. Stitch the rows together. Backstitch at the beginning and end of each row. Press the seams open to reduce bulk at the seam intersections.

7. Zigzag or staystitch the edges of the quilt.

QUILT FINISHING

1. Cut the backing fabric into 2 pieces, each 42" x 55". Stitch the 2 pieces together lengthwise. Trim to 55" x 64".

2. Layer the quilt top with batting (optional) and the pieced backing; baste.

3. Quilt as desired.

4. Trim the backing and batting even with the quilt top.

5. Bind the quilt with the black-print strips.

6. Stitch a label to the quilt back.

SUNSHINE AND FLOWERS

SUNSHINE AND FLOWERS designed by Judy Hooworth and Jane Gibson, 2000, Sydney, Australia, 36" x 45" (88 cm x 110 cm).
Pieced and quilted by Jane Gibson.

• • •

Sunny yellow and blue prints are featured in this delightful quilt with Saturated Crazy blocks set on point.

FINISHED BLOCK SIZE: *5" x 5" (12.5 cm x 12.5 cm)*
DESIGN: *Saturated Crazy*

MATERIALS

42"-wide fabric

- Approximately 1⅜ yds. *total* of assorted yellow scraps at least 1" x 15" for blocks and outer border corner squares
- 1⅛ yds. muslin for block foundations
- ⅝ yd. *total* of assorted blue scraps for sashing and outer border corner squares
- ¼ yd. pink print for sashing joining squares and outer border corner squares
- ¼ yd. blue-and-white lengthwise-striped print for inner border
- ⅝ yd. yellow print for outer border
- 40" x 49" piece of lightweight batting
- 1⅜ yds. fabric for backing
- ⅜ yd. dark blue print for binding

CUTTING INSTRUCTIONS

All measurements include ¼" seam allowances.

From the assorted yellow scraps, cut a *total* of:

- 8 squares, each 2¼" x 2¼". Cut each square in half diagonally to make 16 half-square triangles for the outer border corner squares.

From the muslin, cut:

- 2 strips, each 12" x 42". Crosscut to make:
  - 4 squares, each 12" x 12", for block foundations
  - 1 rectangle, 6½" x 12", for block foundations

- 3 squares, each 9½" x 9½", for setting triangle foundations
- 2 squares, each 5½" x 5½", for corner triangle foundations

From the blue scraps, cut a *total* of:

- 48 strips, each 2" x 5½", for sashing
- 8 squares, each 2⅞" x 2⅞". Cut each square in half diagonally to make 16 half-square triangles for the outer border corner squares.

From the pink print, cut:

- 2 strips, each 2" x 42". Crosscut into 31 squares, each 2" x 2", for sashing joining squares.
- 4 squares, each 2½" x 2½", for outer border corner squares

From the blue-and-white striped fabric, cut:

- 2 strips, each 1" x 28½", for the inner top and bottom borders
- 2 strips, each 1" x 37½", for the inner side borders

From the yellow print, cut:

- 2 strips, each 4" x 28½", for the outer top and bottom borders
- 2 strips, each 4" x 37½", for the outer side borders

From the dark blue print, cut:

- 4 strips, each 2" x 42", for binding

QUILT TOP ASSEMBLY

1. Refer to "Going Crazy" on page 28 to review the instructions for Crazy piecing. Cut the remainder of the yellow scraps into wedge shapes. Sew the wedges to all of the muslin foundation pieces, mixing the prints in each one. Trim the edges of each piece neatly.

2. Trim the pieced 12" squares to 11" x 11". Crosscut each 11" square into 4 blocks, each 5½" x 5½". From the pieced 6½" x 12" rectangle, cut two 5½" x 5½" blocks. Trim the pieced 9½" squares (for setting triangles) to 8½" x 8½". Cut each 8½" square twice diagonally to make 12 quarter-square setting triangles (2 left over). Trim the pieced 5½" squares (for corner triangles) to 4½" x 4½". Cut each square in half diagonally to make 4 half-square triangles for the corners.

3. Referring to the diagram below, stitch the pieced blocks, setting triangles, corner triangles, and blue sashing strips together to make the block rows. Press the seam allowances toward the sashing strips. Stitch the remaining sashing strips and sashing joining squares together to make the sashing rows. Press the seam allow-ances toward the sashing strips. Stitch the sashing rows and block rows together.

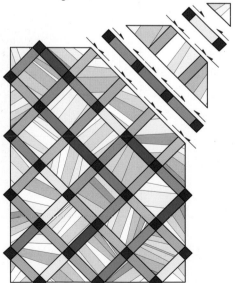

4. Draw a line around the quilt top outer edges that runs through the center of the outer pink sashing joining squares. Trim the quilt edges ¼" from the marked line.

Trim points. Leave ¼" seam allowance.

5. To make the outer border corner squares, stitch 4 yellow and 4 blue half-square triangles to a 2½" pink square as shown. Make 4.

Make 4.

6. Stitch an inner border strip to each outer border strip, matching lengths. Stitch the pieced top and bottom border strips to the top and bottom edges of the quilt top. Press the seam allowances toward the borders. Stitch a pieced outer border corner square to each end of the remaining strips. Stitch the pieced side border strips to the quilt sides. Press the seam allowances toward the borders.

Make 1 top and 1 bottom border.

Make 2 side borders.

QUILT FINISHING

1. Layer the quilt top with batting and the backing; baste.

2. Quilt as desired.

3. Trim the backing and batting even with the quilt top.

4. Bind the quilt with the dark blue strips.

5. Stitch a label to the quilt back.

CRAZY FOR OZ

CRAZY FOR OZ designed by Judy Hooworth, 2000, Sydney, Australia, 59" x 74" (147.5 cm x 185 cm).
Pieced by Karen Fail and quilted by Kerry Adams.

• • •

Stunning black-and-white prints contrast vividly with solid brights in Karen Fail's Uncontrolled Crazy quilt.

Finished Block Size: 6" x 6" (15 cm x 15 cm)
Design: Double-split Uncontrolled Crazy

MATERIALS

42"-wide fabric

- Approximately 2 yds. *total* of assorted black-and-white prints at least 1" x 15" for blocks
- Scraps of assorted solid colors for blocks
- 2 yds. muslin for foundation rectangles
- 6½" x 6½" square *each* of 12 assorted solid colors for single-split sashing strips
- 4½" x 6" rectangle of black-and-white print for single-split sashing joining squares
- ¼ yd. black solid for double-split sashing strips
- 1 yd. red print for double-split sashing strips
- ¼ yd. yellow-and-black print for double-split sashing joining squares
- 2½ yds. black-and-white check for border
- 61" x 76" piece of lightweight batting
- 3½ yds. fabric for backing
- ¾ yd. orange print for binding

CUTTING INSTRUCTIONS

All measurements include ¼" seam allowances.

From the muslin, cut:

- 8 strips, each 7½" x 42". Crosscut into 24 rectangles, each 7½" x 14", for foundations.

From *each* of the 6½" x 6½" squares of assorted solid colors, cut:

- 4 strips, each 1½" x 6½", for single-split sashing strips

From the 4½" x 6" rectangle of black-and-white print, cut:

- 3 strips, each 1½" x 6". Crosscut into 12 squares, each 1½" x 1½", for single-split sashing joining squares.

From the black solid, cut:

- 4 strips, each 1½" x 42". Crosscut into 62 rectangles, each 1½" x 2½", for double-split sashing strips.

From the red print, cut:

- 11 strips, each 2½" x 42". Crosscut into 31 rectangles, each 2½" x 11½", for double-split sashing strips.

From the yellow-and-black print, cut:

- 2 strips, each 2½" x 42". Crosscut into 20 squares, each 2½" x 2½", for double-split sashing joining squares.

From the black-and-white check, cut:

- 2 lengthwise strips, each 6½" x 47½", for the top and bottom borders*
- 2 lengthwise strips, each 6½" x 74½", for the side borders*

From the orange print, cut:

- 7 strips, each 3" x 42", for binding

*Cut the border strips longer if necessary to match the pattern.

QUILT TOP ASSEMBLY

1. Refer to "Going Crazy" on page 28 to review the instructions for Crazy piecing. Cut the black-and-white prints into wedge shapes from 1" to 6" wide and 9" long. Cut the solid-color scraps into narrow wedges ¾" to 2" wide and 9" long. Sew the wedges to the muslin foundation rectangles. Mix the black-and-white prints and values in each rectangle, and add solid-color wedges as desired. Neaten the edges of each piece.

2. Cut each pieced rectangle from step 1 into 2 square blocks, each 6½" x 6½".

3. Stitch 4 pieced blocks, 4 identical 1½" x 6½" sashing strips, and one 1½" x 1½" sashing joining square together as shown. Press the seam allow-ances toward the sashing strips. Make 12.

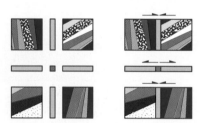

Make 12.

4. Stitch a black 1½" x 2½" rectangle to each end of each red 2½" x 11½" sashing strip.

5. To make the block rows, alternately stitch 4 pieced sashing strips and 3 blocks together, beginning and ending with a sashing strip. Press the seam allowances toward the sashing strips. Make 4 rows.

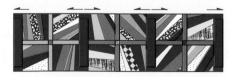

Make 4.

6. To make the sashing rows, alternately stitch 4 yellow-and-black sashing joining squares and 3 pieced sashing strips together, beginning and ending with a joining square. Press the seam allowances toward the sashing strips. Make 5 rows.

7. Alternately stitch the sashing rows and block rows together, beginning and ending with a sashing row. Press the seam allowances toward the sashing rows.

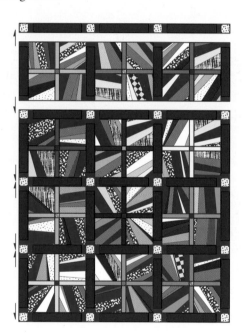

8. Stitch the top and bottom borders to the top and bottom edges of the quilt top. Press the seam allowances toward the borders. Stitch the side borders to the quilt sides. Press the seam allowances toward the borders.

QUILT FINISHING

1. Cut the backing fabric into 2 pieces, each 42" x 63". Stitch the pieces together lengthwise. Trim to 63" x 78".

2. Layer the quilt top with batting and the pieced backing; baste.

3. Quilt as desired.

4. Trim the backing and batting even with the quilt top.

5. Bind the quilt with the orange-print strips.

6. Stitch a label to the quilt back.

PHOTO GALLERY

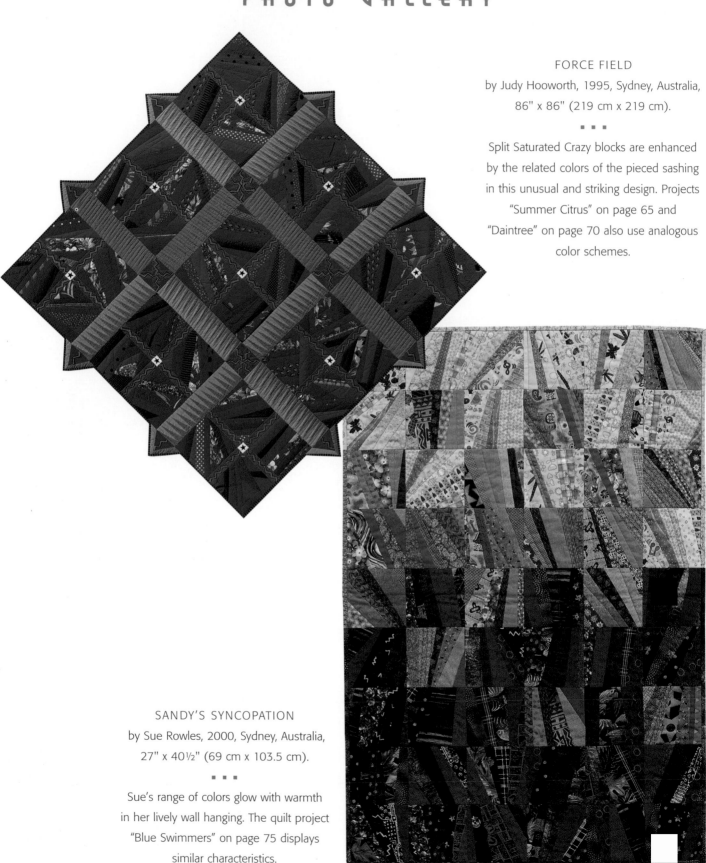

FORCE FIELD
by Judy Hooworth, 1995, Sydney, Australia,
86" x 86" (219 cm x 219 cm).

• • •

Split Saturated Crazy blocks are enhanced
by the related colors of the pieced sashing
in this unusual and striking design. Projects
"Summer Citrus" on page 65 and
"Daintree" on page 70 also use analogous
color schemes.

SANDY'S SYNCOPATION
by Sue Rowles, 2000, Sydney, Australia,
27" x 40½" (69 cm x 103.5 cm).

• • •

Sue's range of colors glow with warmth
in her lively wall hanging. The quilt project
"Blue Swimmers" on page 75 displays
similar characteristics.

COMPOSITION IN RED, YELLOW, AND BLUE

by Judy Hooworth, 1991, Sydney, Australia, 84½" x 84½" (215 cm x 215 cm).

• • •

An arrangement of split Saturated Crazy blocks set on point contrast with the yellow-print sashing and pieced borders.

FLORAL TRELLIS

by Judy Hooworth, 2000, Sydney, Australia, 52" x 52" (135 cm x 135 cm).

• • •

Bright colors from the garden are framed by geometric lattice in this Log Cabin/Ocean Waves block variation. Refer to page 27 for information on the Log Cabin/Ocean Waves block.

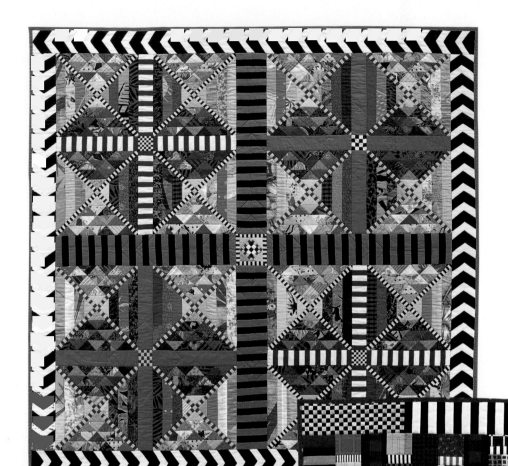

SOUL MUSIC
by Judy Hooworth, 1992, Sydney,
Australia, 65" x 65"
(165 cm x 165 cm).

. . .

Cool colors are combined in a
Log Cabin/Ocean Waves
block variation in a triple-split set.

DOWNTOWN
by Judy Hooworth, 2000, Sydney, Australia,
47" x 60" (119 cm x 153 cm).

. . .

Rectangles of checks and plaids in colorful
variations create a design depicting the
hustle and bustle of the city.

BLOCK OF THE MONTH

Will be drawn at SEPTEMBER 2013 meeting

America's Cup Sailboat - makes one 8" finished block

Submitted by Maren Larsen

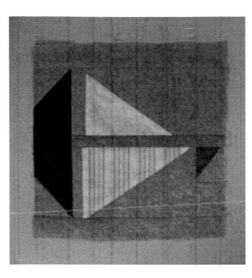

In honor of the America's Cup being held in SF I thought it would be fun to make a sailboat block. It's a bit trickier than I usually put in the block of the month, but if you take your time, it will turn out great.

Sky: 1 rectangle 4" x 6", 1 rectangle 3½" x 1", 1 rectangle 2" x 2½", 1 rectangle 1½" x 2", 1 rectangle 4" x 5½", 1 rectangle 1½"x 4", 1 rectangle 2" x 3½", 2 squares 2" x 2", 2 rectangles 1¼" x 8½""

Large sail: 1 rectangle 4" x 6"
Small sail: 1 rectangle 4" x 5½"
Flag: 1 rectangle 2" x 2½"
Boat: 1 rectangle 2" x 7"
Mast: 1 rectangle 1" x 7"

Place both large sail and sky 4" x 6" rectangles face side up. Use a ruler to cut a diagonal line from the upper left corner to the lower right corner. Sew one set on diagonal to form rectangle and trim to 3½"x 5½". Sew sky rectangle 3½" x 1" to bottom of large sail.

Place both flag and sky rectangle 2" x 2½"face side up. Cut a diagonal from the upper left hand corner. Sew on diagonal, press toward flag and trim to 1 ½"x 2. Sew to sky fabric 1½"x 2". Sew flag unit to top of large sail. Sew to right side of mast.

Place small sail and sky 4" x 5½"rectangles face side up. Use a ruler to cut a rectangle from the upper right corner to the bottom left corner. Trim both straight sides of the sail triangle by ¼". Sew sky rectangle 1½"x 4" to bottom of small sail (the rectangle will extend beyond the sail on the left side, after you sew it onto the sail you will extend the diagonal cut through the sky to form a new triangle). Sew this sail unit onto the sky diagonal to form a rectangle unit and trim to 3½"x 5". Sew sky rectangle 2" x 3½" to top of smaller sail unit. Sew to left side of mast. Press both sail units toward the mast.

At this point you should have a sail unit 7" x 7".

Using the sew and flip method, sew the 2" sky squares diagonally to the ends of the sailboat piece 2" x 7" inches. Trim and press toward the sailboat. Sew to bottom of sail.

Sew sky pieces 1½"x 8½"to sides of sailboat. Congratulations, you should have an unfinished sailboat that measures 8½"x 8½".

For each block you bring to the guild meeting, your name will be entered in the monthly drawing. If your name is drawn you will win all blocks submitted that month. For questions contact Maren Larsen 664-4236.

likes traditional quilting, her favorite quilts are those that create optical illusions. She is a member of a long-standing sewing circle.

Joyce Goode is our Parliamentarian candidate. Joyce has served as Vice President and President and chaired Quiltaway 12. In 2002, she served in Community Outreach. Her quilting interest began with a visit to a quilt show in Monterey. She was so inspired she came back home and took private lessons. Now she is part of 2 sewing circles and has started the Michigan State Baby Quilt Project that she works on every day.

※※

THE SEWCIAL SCENE

CUT, SEW, DONE!!

Saturday, August 24, 2013 - 10am - 4pm

Instructor: *Tish Chung*　　　Fee: $25.00

CUT, SEW, DONE! is easy piecing, no binding and your quilt will be done in no time! This faux cathedral windows is perfect for a variety of themes and fabrics (i.e.: batiks, ethnic fabrics, children's themes, holidays, etc.), is a great stash-buster, and wonderful to make for gifts. And, you can make it any size you want!

EASY CURVED PIECING

Saturday, September 21, 2013 - 10 am - 4 pm

Instructor: *Kenan Shapero*　　　Fee: $25.00

Are you intimidated by the idea of sewing curves? Do they seem too complicated? Learn how easy it is to do free cut curved piecing (no templates needed) and add a new element to your quilts. Bring a variety of fabrics to play with, rotary cutter and mat, and a ruler and we will dive in.

FABRIC CARDS

Saturday, October 19, 2013 - 10 am - 4 pm

Instructor: *Jeanie Low*　　　Fee: $25.00

Make an unforgettable and treasured fabric card. Fabric scraps (batik, cotton, silk, brocade, vintage pieces) go a long way to create a unique card. We'll do some machine applique and a thread dance. This workshop requires a sewing machine that will do a satin stitch.

Please pay when you sign up in advance for Sewcials, or contact Jay Beatty, (415) 647-1283 (jay875@sbcglobal.net). A supply list will be provided when you sign up. *Arrive about 15 minutes* *before the start of the workshop (9:45 am)* to set up and get directions so that we can begin on time. *Please remember that there are no refunds for cancellations. For the comfort of all, please attend Sewcials "fragrance-free." All sewcials are held at the San Francisco Police Academy. Map follows.*

Directions to the Police Academy:

SF Police Academy

SECRETS OF THE BUSH
by Judy Hooworth, 2000, Sydney, Australia,
30" x 50" (75 cm x 125 cm).

• • •

Crazy-pieced blocks depict the linear
patterns of nature in the
Australian landscape.

MARELLA POLKA
by Judy Hooworth, 1999, Sydney, Australia,
58½" x 71½" (148.5 cm x 181.5 cm).
Quilted by Kerry Adams.

• • •

Colorful prints contrast with black-and-white
stripes in this lively combination of
squares and rectangles.

SQUARE DANCE
by Judy Hooworth, 2000, Sydney, Australia,
45½" x 56" (116 cm x 142 cm).

• • •

Yellow Four Patch blocks are framed by
red and blue prints in this lively little quilt.
The large polka dot border print
complements the piecing.

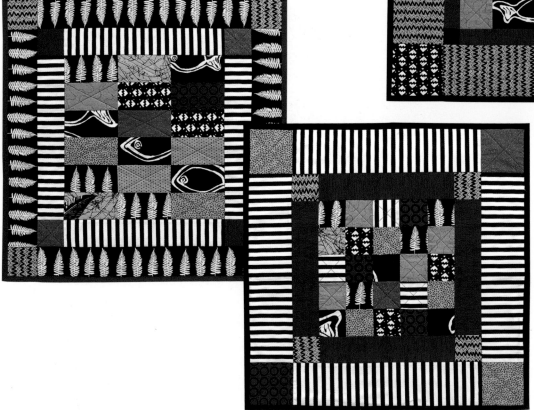

COMBO #1,
COMBO #2, AND
COMBO #3
by Judy Hooworth,
1999, Sydney, Australia,
26" x 26"
(68 cm x 68 cm).

• • •

Sparkling black-and-
white prints contrast
with brights in these
matching quilts.

RAZZLE DAZZLE
by Judy Hooworth, 1992,
Sydney, Australia, 79" x 79"
(200 cm x 200 cm).

. . .

Double-split Log Cabin blocks set
on point create a riot of color.

CROSSROADS
by Judy Hooworth, 2000,
Sydney, Australia, 43½" x 43½"
(111 cm x 111 cm).

. . .

The split Courthouse Steps blocks
(a variation of the Log Cabin block)
are surrounded by graphic pieced
borders in this dramatic design.

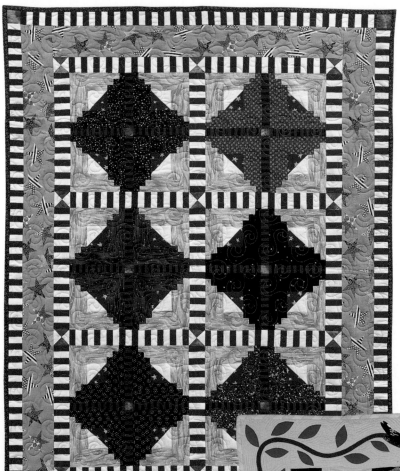

STRIPES 'N STARS
by Judy Hooworth, 2000, Sydney, Australia,
48" x 65" (122 cm x 165.5 cm).
Quilted by Kerry Adams.

• • •

Bold red-and-white stripes enliven
the starry Log Cabin block.

CURRAWONGS
by Judy Hooworth, 1990, Sydney, Australia,
48" x 53" (122 cm x 135 cm).
Photographed by Geoff Hirst, Sydney,
Australia.

• • •

This quilt was inspired by the
black-and-white currawongs that visit my
garden. Black-and-white prints contrast
with solid yellow in Log Cabin blocks
with red and blue center squares.
The Straight-Furrows quilt design is
surrounded with an appliqué border.

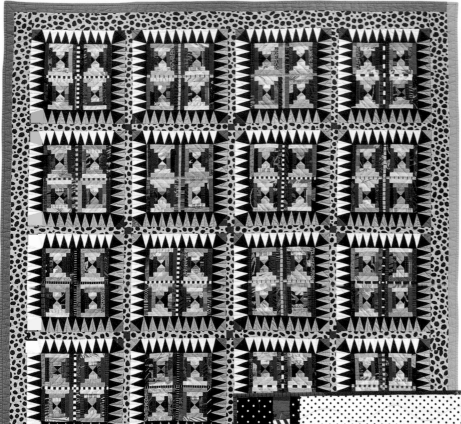

PHOENIX
by Judy Hooworth, 1990,
Sydney, Australia, 74½" x 74½"
(189 cm x 189 cm).

• • •

The split Courthouse Steps blocks are
surrounded by pieced borders and
vivid black-and-yellow leopard-print
sashing in this dramatic quilt.

RAINBOW CRAZY
by Judy Hooworth, 1998,
Sydney, Australia, 61" x 67"
(154 cm x 169 cm).

• • •

Bright prints are combined in this
Uncontrolled Crazy block quilt set in
a basket weave arrangement.

CRAZY RHYTHM
by Judy Hooworth, 1994,
Sydney, Australia, 85" x 85"
(215 cm x 215 cm).
▪ ▪ ▪
Split red and yellow Uncontrolled
Crazy blocks have been set on point
and accented with purple and yellow
zigzag-print sashing.

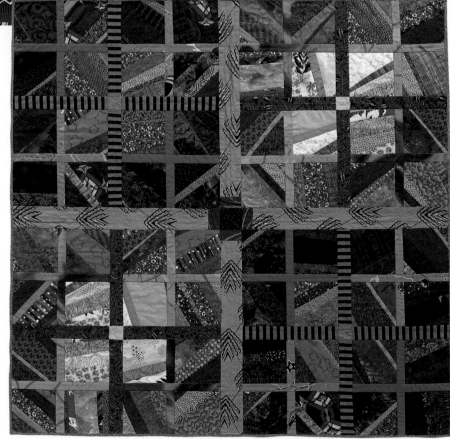

AMETHYST WINDOWS
by Judy Hooworth, 2000, Sydney,
Australia, 39½" x 39½"
(100 cm x 100 cm).
Pieced and quilted by Carolyn Sullivan.
▪ ▪ ▪
Oranges and violets contrast vividly
in this triple-split set of controlled
crazy blocks.

BIBLIOGRAPHY

Beyer, Jinny. *The Quilters' Album of Blocks and Borders*. McLean, Va.: EPM Publications Inc., 1980.

Denton, Susan and Barbara Macey. *Quiltmaking*. Melbourne, Australia: Thomas Nelson Australia, 1987.

Hughes, Robert. *Amish. The Art of the Quilt*. London: Phaidon Press, 1994.

Lauer, David A. *Design Basics*. San Francisco: Holt, Rinehart and Winston, 1979.

Leman, Mary, and Judy Martin. *Log Cabin Quilts*. Denver, Colo.: Moon Over the Mountain Publishing Co., 1980.

_____ . *Taking the Math out of Making Patchwork Quilts*. Denver, Colo.: Moon Over the Mountain Publishing Co., Inc., 1982.

ABOUT THE AUTHOR

JUDY HOOWORTH is a leading Australian quiltmaker, but she first started out as an art teacher after training in art and illustration at the National Art School in Sydney, Australia. In the 1960s and 1970s, she saw quilts in glossy American magazines and began making them, primarily learning by doing. She later worked with Noreen Dunn to make quilts on commission through their partnership, Quiltek.

Even while working on commissioned pieces, Judy always kept an interest in contemporary quilts and made her own original work. Over the years, Judy has exhibited in the annual exhibition of the New South Wales Quilters' Guild and has been involved in most of Australia's contemporary quilt exhibitions. She was a key organizer of the New Quilt exhibition of contemporary quilts held at the Manly Art Gallery and Museum. In 1994, Judy won the Quilters' Guild N.S.W. Scholarship, and in 1995 she received a professional development grant from the visual arts/crafts fund of the Australia Council. In 1992, one of Judy's quilts was selected for the exhibition Visions—The Art of the Quilt, San Diego.

Judy has also successfully entered quilts in Quilt National with "Composition in Yellow" in 1993, "Mothers/Daughters #6: Lines of Communication" in 1999, and "Life Force" in 2001. Judy has taught quiltmaking throughout Australia, New Zealand, Germany, and the U.S. and continues to make her own art quilts. *Razzle Dazzle Quilts* is her second book for Martingale & Company. Her first, which was co-authored with Margaret Rolfe in 1999, is titled *Spectacular Scraps: A Simple Approach to Stunning Quilts*.

NEW AND BESTSELLING TITLES FROM

America's Best-Loved Craft & Hobby Books™

America's Best-Loved Quilt Books®

QUILTING
from That Patchwork Place®, an imprint of Martingale & Company™

Appliqué
Artful Appliqué
Colonial Appliqué
Red and Green: An Appliqué Tradition
Rose Sampler Supreme
Your Family Heritage: Projects in
   Appliqué

Baby Quilts
Appliqué for Baby
The Quilted Nursery
Quilts for Baby: Easy as ABC
More Quilts for Baby: Easy as ABC
Even More Quilts for Baby: Easy as ABC

Holiday Quilts
Easy and Fun Christmas Quilts
Favorite Christmas Quilts from That
   Patchwork Place
Paper Piece a Merry Christmas
A Snowman's Family Album Quilt
Welcome to the North Pole

Learning to Quilt
Basic Quiltmaking Techniques for:
   Borders and Bindings
   Curved Piecing
   Divided Circles
   Eight-Pointed Stars
   Hand Appliqué
   Machine Appliqué
   Strip Piecing
The Joy of Quilting
The Quilter's Handbook
Your First Quilt Book (or it should be!)

Paper Piecing
50 Fabulous Paper-Pieced Stars
A Quilter's Ark
Easy Machine Paper Piecing
Needles and Notions
Paper-Pieced Curves
Show Me How to Paper Piece

Rotary Cutting
101 Fabulous Rotary-Cut Quilts
365 Quilt Blocks a Year Perpetual
   Calendar
Fat Quarter Quilts
Lap Quilting Lives!
Quick Watercolor Quilts
Quilts from Aunt Amy
Spectacular Scraps
Time-Crunch Quilts

Small & Miniature Quilts
Bunnies By The Bay Meets Little Quilts
Celebrate! with Little Quilts
Easy Paper-Pieced Miniatures
Little Quilts All Through the House

CRAFTS
From Martingale & Company

300 Papermaking Recipes
The Art of Handmade Paper and
   Collage
The Art of Stenciling
Creepy Crafty Halloween
Gorgeous Paper Gifts
Grow Your Own Paper
Stamp with Style
Wedding Ribbonry

KNITTING
From Martingale & Company

Comforts of Home
Fair Isle Sweaters Simplified
Knit It Your Way
Simply Beautiful Sweaters
Two Sticks and a String
The Ultimate Knitter's Guide
Welcome Home: Kaffe Fassett

COLLECTOR'S COMPASS™
From Martingale & Company

20th Century Glass
'50s Decor
Barbie® Doll
Jewelry

Coming to *Collector's Compass* Spring 2001:

20th Century Dinnerware
American Coins
Movie Star Collectibles
'60s Decor

10/00